AF790207

SpringerBriefs in Psychology

SpringerBriefs in Behavioral Criminology

Series editor: Vincent B. Van Hasselt

For further volumes:
http://www.springer.com/series/10850

Tia A. Hoffer • Joy Lynn E. Shelton

Suicide Among Child Sex Offenders

Springer

Tia A. Hoffer
Federal Bureau of Investigation
Quantico, VA, USA

Joy Lynn E. Shelton
Federal Bureau of Investigation
Quantico, VA, USA

ISSN 2192-8363 ISSN 2192-8371 (electronic)
ISBN 978-1-4614-5936-1 ISBN 978-1-4614-5937-8 (eBook)
DOI 10.1007/978-1-4614-5937-8
Springer New York Heidelberg Dordrecht London

Library of Congress Control Number: 2012951415

© Springer Science+Business Media New York 2013
This work is subject to copyright. All rights are reserved by the Publisher, whether the whole or part of the material is concerned, specifically the rights of translation, reprinting, reuse of illustrations, recitation, broadcasting, reproduction on microfilms or in any other physical way, and transmission or information storage and retrieval, electronic adaptation, computer software, or by similar or dissimilar methodology now known or hereafter developed. Exempted from this legal reservation are brief excerpts in connection with reviews or scholarly analysis or material supplied specifically for the purpose of being entered and executed on a computer system, for exclusive use by the purchaser of the work. Duplication of this publication or parts thereof is permitted only under the provisions of the Copyright Law of the Publisher's location, in its current version, and permission for use must always be obtained from Springer. Permissions for use may be obtained through RightsLink at the Copyright Clearance Center. Violations are liable to prosecution under the respective Copyright Law.
The use of general descriptive names, registered names, trademarks, service marks, etc. in this publication does not imply, even in the absence of a specific statement, that such names are exempt from the relevant protective laws and regulations and therefore free for general use.
While the advice and information in this book are believed to be true and accurate at the date of publication, neither the authors nor the editors nor the publisher can accept any legal responsibility for any errors or omissions that may be made. The publisher makes no warranty, express or implied, with respect to the material contained herein.

Printed on acid-free paper

Springer is part of Springer Science+Business Media (www.springer.com)

Contents

Abstract

The Federal Bureau of Investigation (FBI) Behavioral Analysis Unit (BAU) III – Crimes Against Children reviewed and analyzed 106 male Child Sex Offenders (CSOs) who committed suicide during the course of a child sex crime investigation. Of the 106 CSOs, 79% were child pornography traders/collectors, 43% were child molesters, 21% were travelers, and 18% were child pornography producers. Analyses also revealed that nearly all were Caucasian and the majority were married, employed, and died via self-inflicted gunshot wound. Of particular interest was that in 26% of the cases, the offender killed himself within 48 hours of his awareness of the investigation, and in nearly half of the known cases, the offender had past/current military service and a criminal history. In addition, 68% left a suicide note, which is substantially higher than the general suicide population. Analysis of the notes revealed common aspects and themes including cognitive distortions, burdensomeness, shame, and self-blame. The most frequently cited reason for the suicide in the note was the child sex crime investigation. Awareness of this potentially high-risk population may better inform the law enforcement, corrections, and mental health communities of the unique risk factors for suicide among CSOs and provide a more effective crisis response.

I. Introduction

Little empirical research exists confirming that child sex offenders (CSO)[1] are at higher risk for suicide (Byrne, Lurigio, & Pimentel, 2009; Hoffer, Shelton, Behnke, & Erdberg, 2010). Nevertheless, law enforcement agencies around the country anecdotally report cases in which an investigation of a child sex crime abruptly ended due to the suicide of the offender.[2] Many CSOs experience high levels of fear, anxiety, shame, and helplessness during the course of an investigation and are often concerned about their future as it relates to their family, work, and reputation (Hoffer et al., 2010; Lanning, 2010). Feeling stigmatized, they might see themselves as a burden to society, having nothing to contribute (Hoffer et al.). They may also believe that disclosure of this information will humiliate and thus burden their family. Motivations for suicide among CSOs are diverse but often include regaining control of a situation that they perceive as helpless and uncertain (e.g., escaping prison time or preventing the disclosure of additional victims) (Hoffer et al.).

Although law enforcement personnel are neither trained nor required to assess an offender's suicidality, awareness of suicide among this population of offenders may mitigate the risk of suicide and enhance operational strategies, including officer safety (Hoffer et al., 2010). Additionally, analyses of these cases may give law enforcement empirically based data to support seizing the offenders' weapons for safety purposes or to argue for the detention of an offender after arrest in order to evaluate his vulnerability to suicide.

---

[1] The term child sex offender (CSO) used here indicates an adult who was being investigated for a sex crime against a child(ren) at the time of his death. The pronouns, he/him/his, are used throughout this document since the BAU sample of CSOs was composed of all males. The child sex crime(s) included the receiving, possessing, distributing, or producing of child pornography, traveling to have sex with a minor, or sexually molesting a child(ren). Due to the suicides of the CSOs occurring early in the investigations, the majority of the sample was never convicted.

[2] For many of the CSOs referenced, there was probable cause to seize evidence in a search or arrest warrant. In some cases, a "knock and talk" was conducted when there was insufficient probable cause for a search or arrest warrant at a specific location or on the offender. A knock and talk involves law enforcement knocking on the offender's residence and asking for consent to interview him and/or review his computer for any evidence of illegal activity.

T.A. Hoffer and J.L.E. Shelton, *Suicide Among Child Sex Offenders*,
SpringerBriefs in Psychology, DOI 10.1007/978-1-4614-5937-8_1,
© Springer Science+Business Media New York 2013

II. Literature Review

a. General Suicide Research

The term "suicide" is defined in the Merriam-Webster Collegiate Dictionary as "the act of killing oneself voluntarily and intentionally" (2004, p. 1249). Various data have been reported regarding the prevalence of suicide among the general population. A 2007 United States report on suicide highlights incidence and prevalence rates, as well as its impact on society at large (McIntosh, 2010). Suicide is considered the eleventh leading cause of death for people in the United States. In 2007, 34,598 people committed suicide (approximately 1 death every 15.2 minutes). Males were 3.6 times more likely than females to take their own lives. Overall, the use of firearms was the most common method of suicide (N=17,352). Additionally, the risk for suicide has also been analyzed among various subpopulations. According to research, suicide rates among adolescent youth, the elderly, and military members are higher than those in the general population (Bryan, Cukrowicz, West, & Morrow, 2010; Joiner, 2010; Kang & Bullman, 2008; McIntosh, 2002).

Suicide impacts not only close family and friends but also those who hear about the suicide. For every person who commits suicide, there are approximately six survivors, a total of 4.6 million people, described as family and friends of the deceased (McIntosh, 2010). Surviving family members and friends of the offender are often left with questions and want to understand why he/she chose to commit suicide. A suicide note left by the individual is often the only source of this information. There is a common misconception that most people leave a suicide note. Joiner (2005) reports that leaving a suicide note occurs in only about 25% of suicides, which is rather uncommon among the general suicide population (Joiner, 2010).

Even in the midst of suicidal thoughts, people typically have an equally and usually greater need to preserve life. This distinction is important, as one-third of the US population has felt suicidal at some point in their life; however, only 0.01% of the population actually die by suicide (McIntosh, 2010; Paykel, Myers, Lindenthal, & Tanner, 1974). So how do individuals get to the point of ending their lives? The vast research on

T.A. Hoffer and J.L.E. Shelton, *Suicide Among Child Sex Offenders*,
SpringerBriefs in Psychology, DOI 10.1007/978-1-4614-5937-8_2,

© Springer Science+Business Media New York 2013

suicide has produced a variety of theories on suicide risk factors. Beginning with the seminal works of Shneidman (1987), the cubic model explained factors related to suicide and incorporated three factors impacting suicidal behavior: (1) press (e.g., external events that impinge on the individual), (2) pain (e.g., thwarted psychological needs such as autonomy or avoidance of humiliation), and (3) perturbation (e.g., state of being upset and possibly a cognitive constriction). Thereafter, other psychologists expanded the understanding of the dynamics of suicide based on their clinical work and research (Bongar, 2002; Jobes, 2006; Joiner, 2005; Maris, Berman, & Silverman, 2000; Silverman, Bongar, Berman, & Maris, 1999).

From the research, specific factors subsumed in the affective, cognitive, behavioral, and alcohol/drug categories have been consistently reported to increase an individual's risk for suicide. Individuals who are less capable of controlling their emotions, including feelings of depression, anxiety, and "psychache,"[1] have increased risk for suicide (Chance, Kaslow, & Baldwin, 1994; Harrington, Fudge, Rutter, Pickles, & Hill, 1990; MacLeod, Williams, & Linehan, 1992). They tend to be more temperamental, unpleasant, submissive, and easily aroused (Mehrabian & Weinstein, 1985). From the cognitive realm, there is an increased risk for suicide by individuals who experience greater helplessness, hopelessness, perfectionism, irrational beliefs, and a weaker reason for living. In addition, those who have a greater external locus of control[2] are also at increased risk because they expect negative outcomes, think things will never change, and are less able to come up with alternative, more appropriate solutions (Beautrais, Joyce, & Mulder, 1999; Blatt, 1995; Cole, 1989; Kehrer & Linehan, 1996; Linehan, Goodstein, Nielsen, & Chiles, 1983; MacLeod et al., 1992; Schotte & Clum, 1987; Woods, Silverman, Gentilini, Cunningham, & Grieger, 1991). Westefield et al. (2000) stated that "…ineffective belief systems and weak problem-solving skills mean that suicidal individuals lack the personal resources they need when they experience strong negative feelings" (pp. 451).

The American Association of Suicidology (2003) presented the main risk factors exhibited by individuals who are considering suicide through a mnemonic device, IS PATH WARM (ideation, substance abuse, purposelessness, anxiety, trapped, hopelessness, withdrawal, anger, recklessness, mood changes). Additionally, the literature consistently reports various risk factors for suicide to include mental disorders, past suicide attempts, social isolation, family conflict, unemployment, and physical illness (Van Orden et al., 2010).

The vast majority of people who die by suicide (i.e., approximately 95%) suffer from a mental disorder (Cavanagh, Carson, Sharpe, & Lawrie, 2003). It is often assumed that the remaining 5% suffer from previously undetected mental disorders (Ernst et al., 2004). In addition, certain mental disorders correlate with higher risk for suicidal behavior compared to others. For example, bipolar disorder presents a

---

[1] "Psychache" is defined as intolerable emotional or psychological pain that cannot be terminated by previously utilized coping mechanisms (Shneidman, 1993).

[2] Julian Rotter (1966) developed the idea that individuals typically believe that their destiny or situations are controlled or influenced either by themselves (internal locus control) or outside factors (external locus of control).

15-fold increased risk for suicide (Harris & Barraclough, 1997) as compared to a major depressive disorder with suicide rates between 2% and 6% (Bostwick & Pankratz, 2000). Studies examining mental disorders and suicides reveal that the vast majority of individuals diagnosed with a mental disorder do not die by suicide (Van Orden et al., 2010).

Research supports the theory that individuals who have also been diagnosed with a personality disorder have an increased risk for suicidal behavior (Duberstein & Conwell, 1997; Kullgren, Tengstrown, & Grann, 1998). Personality disorders indicate an enduring pattern of characterological traits that deviate from the expected behaviors of the individual's culture. Personality disorders manifest in two or more of the following: perception and interpretation (cognition), emotional response (affect), interpersonal function, and impulse control. The pattern of behavior is stable and pervasive across a broad range of personal and social situations, which results in clinically significant distress and impairment in important areas such as social situations or occupational settings. The pattern can be traced back to adolescence and early adulthood. The Millon Clinical Multiaxial Inventory III (MCMI-III; Millon, Millon, Davis, & Grossman, 1997) personality scales: schizoid (scale 1), avoidant (scale 2), dependent (scale 3), and passive-aggressive (scale 8) were elevated among those who had suicidal ideations and attempts (Hull, Range, & Goggin, 1992; Lall, Bonger, Johnson, Jain, & Mittauer, 1999; McCann & Suess, 1988). In addition, antisocial personality disorder (ASPD) and borderline personality disorder (BPD) were associated with suicide among the general population (Duberstein & Conwell; Patrick, Zempolich, & Levenston, 1997; Verona, Patrick, & Joiner, 2001).

An earlier analysis of suicides by Baechler (1979) presented four reasons why someone chooses to die by suicide: (1) suicides which occur during the commission of a crime, (2) suicides which allow the individual to maintain honor and/or save face, (3) suicides which occur while a person is engaged in high-risk behavior, and (4) suicides which are the result of flight or escape from an intolerable situation (Shneidman, 2001). People who engage in the escapist suicide act often experience shame, guilt, fear, and worthlessness.

The suicide trajectory model (Stillion, McDowell, & May, 1989) indicates that the suicidal individual experiences a triggering event that becomes the last straw resulting in the suicidal behavior. The model includes biological factors, such as a predisposition to commit suicide; psychological factors including depression, hopelessness, helplessness, low self-esteem, and poor coping abilities; cognitive factors such as cognitive rigidity and cognitive distortions; and environmental factors including losses, negative events, poor family experiences, and the presence of firearms.

Strayer and Marzani (2011) reported a distinction between subjects who engage with law enforcement. Some "want to die" and others are "ready and willing to die." Individuals who want to die might engage in suicidal behaviors to reach their goal. For others, suicide might not be their main goal, but they may be willing and ready to die as a result of their potentially high-risk action(s). Researchers, such as Joiner (2005), argue that the person who commits suicide must have the courage to do so, while others believe that suicide is the product of fear and an escape from pain:

"Suicide sometimes proceeds from cowardice, but not always; for cowardice sometimes prevents it; since as many live because they are afraid to die as die because they are afraid to live" (Colton, 1829, p. 156). A CSO interviewed by the Federal Bureau of Investigation's (FBI) Behavioral Analysis Unit (BAU) stated he was too afraid to kill himself and could not think of a way to commit suicide that was guaranteed to end his life without being painful.

An awareness of risk factors does not allow for accurately predicting a person's eventual suicide given the converging internal and external factors in an individual's life (Joiner, 2005). Risk factors are only indicators of a possible suicide. Threatening suicide, talking or writing about suicide, and buying a weapon are often considered warning signs and imply imminent risk for suicide, demanding specific interventions (American Association of Suicidology, 2003). Even exhibiting these types of risk factors does not predict an individual's suicide. Researchers believe an individual's resiliency – degree of resourcefulness – is key to coping with stressors and thus avoiding suicide. People with greater resilience have protective factors, such as positive emotions, that ward off mental disorders like depression or anxiety and decrease vulnerability to suicide (Johnson, Gooding, Wood, & Tarrier, 2010). Therefore, resiliency may be the key component that enables CSOs who do not choose suicide to cope with the shame they experience as a result of the investigation.

Joiner's (2005) Interpersonal-Psychological Theory (IPT) of suicidal behavior has received an increasing amount of empirical support. Joiner's model proposes that three important features must be present for an individual to die by suicide: (1) perceived burdensomeness, (2) thwarted belonging, and (3) acquired capability for suicide. Joiner proposes that these three domains can be used to determine not only who desires to die by suicide but also who is most capable of lethal self-injury (Selby et al., 2010). These two important concepts of the IPT (desire and capability) are important especially when considering that despite the approximately 15% of the US population who seriously consider suicide, only 1.4% actually die by suicide (Nock, Borges, Bromet, Cha, et al., 2008; Nock, Borges, Bromet, Alnoso, et al., 2008). This disparity suggests that something prevents suicidal people from dying by suicide, despite their desire to do so.

Perceived burdensomeness and thwarted belonging are two of the three domains which constitute one's "desire for death" (i.e., *why* someone would die by suicide) (Selby et al., 2010). Perceived burdensomeness is the sense that the individual feels he is a burden to others, does not contribute to a group, and poses a liability to the group's well-being or safety. His feeling of an inability to make meaningful contributions to society also adds to his sense of burdensomeness and allows him to assume that his death is worth more to others than his life (Selby et al.).

Individuals with thwarted belongingness have an unmet need to belong which comes from a lack of frequent and positive social interactions as well as feelings of not being cared about by others (Baumeister & Leary, 1995; Selby et al.). They lack important connections to others and previously meaningful relationships have been strained or lost. Some individuals may have made attempts to belong, but various obstacles have prevented them from fitting in and connecting with others. Thwarted belongingness can be applied to those individuals who are physically isolated as well as to those who have contact with family and friends. In many cases, the individuals who have frequent contact with others feel they are not genuinely connected to the group and that their contributions are insignificant at best. Various studies have confirmed the concept that thwarted belongingness is highly correlated with suicidal ideation, suicide attempts, and completed suicide (Conner, Britton, Sworts, & Joiner, 2007; Joiner, Hollar, & Van Orden, 2006; Van Orden, Witte, Gordon, Bender, & Joiner, 2008).

The third feature, acquired capability, is the degree to which an individual is able to actually commit suicide (i.e., *who* can commit suicide). The act of suicide is extremely fear inducing and often pain inducing; therefore, habituation to the fear and pain involved is required for suicidal behavior (Joiner, 2005; Van Orden, et al., 2008). Joiner uses the example of jumping out of a plane (skydiving) or parachute training to illustrate this concept. With each jump, the individual feels significantly less terror. Acquired capability develops through a variety of experiences to include medical problems, surgeries, drug use, exposure to violence, military experience, past suicidal attempts, and repeated tattooing and piercing (Joiner). The impact of these experiences does not fade quickly; once in place, acquired capability is relatively static and does not come and go over time (Joiner). Acquired capability for suicide separates individuals who desire to die by suicide from those who actually commit suicide. Although each feature of Joiner's IPT is necessary for suicide, each feature in isolation is not sufficient. Joiner proposes that only when both desire and capability coexist will suicide occur.

Suicide has also been analyzed among various subpopulations to include active military members and veterans. Previous studies have indicated that individuals with military service may be at increased risk for suicidal behavior (Kaplan, Huguet, McFarland, & Newsome, 2007). Recent research has proposed that military service increases one's acquired capability since combat and training exposes an individual to pain, fear, and death (Selby et al., 2010). Combat experience may help an individual develop a sense of "invincibility," which can lead him/her to engage in more risky behaviors and develop a greater sense of fearlessness. War zone violence is likely to be the greatest contributor to acquired capability. Recent studies have shown that military training alone can increase one's ability to commit suicide (Bryan et al., 2010; Selby et al.). During military training repeated injuries, use of dangerous weapons, simulated combat activities, and other intense situations are common. This can decrease one's fear of death and one's sensitivity to pain (Joiner, 2005; Selby et al.). Access, familiarity, and comfort level with firearms is also likely to be higher among military members. If one is trained in firearms, then using a gun to commit suicide may not invoke as much fear as other potential methods (Selby et al.). In addition, military members are more likely to own a personal gun than are members of the general population (Hepburn, Miller, Azrael, & Hemenway, 2007). The nature of military service decreases one's fear of death through the reoccurring experience of pain and possible death. This habituation process (acquired capability) may extend to suicide if suicidal ideation (the desire to die) is present (Selby et al.).

Risk for suicide is not limited to those in an active duty status. Veterans are also at risk for suicide due to increased problems with families, difficulties at work, chronic combat injuries, and depression. For example, depression causes difficulty dealing with loneliness and lack of connection, maintaining an occupation, and it contributes to feelings of worthlessness (Koren, Norman, Cohen, Berman, & Klein, 2005). Post-traumatic stress disorder (PTSD), a common disorder among military veterans, is strongly associated with suicidal behavior (Kessler, 2000). Many of the clinical features of PTSD, such as agitation, insomnia, and nightmares, are also identified risk factors for suicide.

In addition, veterans can experience difficulties integrating back into civilian life, which can increase feelings of burdensomeness and lack of belonging. Whether veterans are physically or psychologically injured upon discharge or retirement, they may lack a sense of purpose and may feel they are a burden on society. Burdensomeness may be increased if one abandons or is expelled from the military. A recent study of soldiers who died by suicide found that involuntary discharge was a significant risk factor for suicide when compared to those who completed their military service (Thoresen & Mehlum, 2006).

While among the general population suicide is the 11th most frequent cause of death, inmates in state and federal prison have higher rates of suicide than the general population. Maruschak (2004) reported that suicide is the third leading cause of death for inmates. Among a sample of inmates in a study by Lamis, Langhinrichsen-Rohling, and Simpler (2008), personality disorders were associated with suicide proneness, especially borderline and schizotypal personality disorders. The behaviors exhibited in individuals with borderline personality disorders included instability in their interpersonal relationships, increased impulsivity, and suicidal behaviors. Among individuals with schizotypal personality disorder, odd or bizarre cognitive functioning influenced their perception that the world was unsafe, causing them to feel greater distress. A finding among this study was that inmates scoring higher on the sadistic (aggressive) scale on the MCMI-III were more likely to be cruel, angry, violent, demeaning, and manipulative. They more frequently spent more time in isolation, and therefore, developed less supportive relationships with others. They also indicated greater signs of suicide proneness and distress. Interestingly, the study found that increased signs of obsessive-compulsive personality disorder contained symptoms of psychological distress as well, possibly due to the individual's rigidity, inflexibility with others, and expectations of perfectionism (Lamis et al. 2008).

b. Suicide Notes

Suicide notes are considered to be an excellent archival source of direct information about the individual who died by suicide (Leenaars & Balance, 1984) and are "windows to the mind of the deceased" (Leenaars, 2004, p. 84). Among the general suicide population, the percentage of people who leave a suicide note ranges from 15% to 55% (Callanan & Davis, 2009; Joiner, 2010; O'Donnell, Farmer, & Catalan,

1993). O'Donnell et al. (1993) found among a sample of 242 probable suicides, 15% (36) left at least one suicide note. In a sample of 621 suicides over a 10-year span (480 males; 141 females), 37.2% left suicide notes (Callanan & Davis). From this study, individuals living alone were 2.5 times more likely to leave a suicide note, were more likely to be depressed and/or socially isolated, and were less likely to have made a prior suicide threat. Joiner (2010) reports that 25% is an average percentage of individuals who die by suicide who leave a suicide note. Ho, Yip, Chiu, and Halliday (1998) report that when individuals leave a suicide note, the suicide act does not tend to be a random phenomenon.

Some researchers have analyzed the similarities and differences among those individuals who leave notes and those who do not. Shneidman (1996) theorized that, in general, different samples of individuals who died by suicide have greater commonalities than differences, including being stressed by unmet psychological needs, feelings of hopeless or helpless, feeling ambivalent, and having cognitive constriction.[1] In addition, the individual may be seeking a solution to a perceived problem, communicating his/her intention to commit suicide, attempting to escape, and/or becoming unconscious to avoid unbearable psychache.

Black and Lester (1995) found no significant differences in their sample based on gender or age among the suicide notes they examined. In a study by Foster (2003), no statistically significant differences were found between individuals who left a note prior to their suicide and those who did not. The variables examined were age, sex, marital status, previous history of deliberate self-harm, and contact with a primary care physician or mental health professional.

Some studies have reported differences among samples based on gender, age, and method. Lester (1990) and Chynoweth (1977) indicated that the following are more likely to leave a suicide note: predominantly younger individuals, women, elderly, and those who used medication, poison, or a firearm as their suicide method. Individuals who were mentally disturbed were less likely to leave a note. More recently, Ho et al. (1998) examined 769 individuals who died by suicide (461 males and 308 females). The group of subjects that left a suicide note was more frequently young females; individuals with non-widowed marital status, who reported no prior suicide attempts or prior mental illness; and those with religious beliefs. Additionally, individuals who used suicide methods that were easily available, such as jumping or cutting their wrists, were less likely to leave a suicide note (Ho et al.).

Incorporating a method of analysis initially used by Shneidman and Farberow (1960) and Darbonne (1969) categorized suicide notes from 156 individuals based on five general categories, including to whom the note was addressed, reasons for the suicide, emotional expressions, content expressed by the suicide writer, and the overall tone of the suicide note. Darbonne found that the individuals who wrote suicide notes did not typically discuss issues related to finances and did not indicate

---

[1] Cognitive constriction is a term that was introduced by Edwin Shneidman to describe the suicidal individual's state of mind as a narrowing of one's focus and includes all-or-nothing (dichotomous) thinking. The individual is unable to consider other alternatives to overcome the "psychache" they are experiencing and subsequently see the only solution being suicide (Shneidman, 1996).

confusion or bizarre psychotic thoughts. Results indicated that younger individuals (ages 20–39), who wrote a suicide note prior to committing suicide, more frequently expressed feelings of rejection and difficulty in coping with problems in their interpersonal relationships. The younger individuals did not comment on illnesses or pain, and they often internalized blame and guilt while expressing self-depreciation. The group of individuals between 40 and 49 years of age more frequently endorsed themes related to the demands of life, being tired or bored, and wanting to escape. This group often focused on obtaining forgiveness from God and expressed hopelessness that the future would change for the better. Individuals in the 50–59-year age group, who wrote notes prior to committing suicide, rarely offered a reason for the suicide, and the tone of the notes was less emotional. They often conveyed practical information in their suicide notes. The authors theorized that individuals in this age group have experienced failing health and were more rational in their decision to die by suicide. Finally, the individuals 60 years and older more frequently reported reasons as to why they committed suicide, which included illness, pain, physical disability, loneliness, and isolation. They expressed feelings of sadness and a desire for forgiveness from identified person(s). Although this group expressed a greater sense of positive self-image and less self-depreciation and guilt, they reported being rejected by others (Darbonne).

Similarly, Leenaars and Balance (1984) conducted a study of 52 suicide notes (48 from suicide and 4 from suicide attempters). The mean age of the sample was 42, and the range was 18–74 years of age. The sample was divided into two groups: under 42 years of age and over 42 years of age, with 25 suicide notes in each group. Results of the study indicated that the younger group was more self-critical, harsher toward themselves, and expressed less self-worth than the older group. In addition, the younger group more frequently referred to others and expressed positive and negative feelings about them.

A number of studies examined themes that individuals often expressed in their suicide notes, such as blame toward self and others, consideration of others, anger, low self-esteem, difficulty coping, obtaining forgiveness, taking control, and pessimism (Bhatia, Verma, & Murty, 2006; Darbonne, 1969; Foster, 2003; Leenaars & Balance, 1984; Lester, Wood, William, & Haines, 2004; Linn & Lester, 1996; McClelland, Reicher, & Both, 2000). McClelland et al. (2000) reported that the concept of blame was the most frequently cited theme within their sample of 172 suicide notes, with 88% of the subjects mentioning blame in their notes. In addition, Linn and Lester reported the presence of 15 characteristics to include: sparing the feelings of others, blaming oneself, blaming others, clear anger, subtle anger, low self-esteem, grief-stricken widow(er), feeling defeated/overwhelmed, feeling hopeless/helpless, unable to show feelings, feeling unworthy, having an incurable disease, performance failure, feeling sorry for oneself, and a failed relationship. Foster found six themes were more commonly present in their sample of suicides notes. The themes included apology/shame (74%), love for those left behind (60%), life too much to bear (48%), instructions regarding practical affairs postmortem (36%), hopelessness/nothing to live for (21%), and advice for those left behind (21%).

Based on Joiner's IPT model, individuals who left a suicide note(s) often included statements supporting the model's three components: lack of belonging, perceived burdensomeness, and acquired capability (Joiner, 2005). Joiner, Pettit, Walker, Voelz, and Cruz (2002) examined how perceived burdensomeness relates to suicidality. They included five dimensions: sense of burdensomeness, regulating emotion, regulating interpersonal relations, degree of emotional pain, and a sense of helplessness. In their study, 20 suicide notes from those who attempted and 20 notes from those who completed suicide were examined. Their results revealed some support that burdensomeness or a feeling that one is a liability to one's loved ones correlates with those who completed suicide. Joiner et al. (2002) found that those who have greater burdensomeness chose more lethal methods of suicide. Higher lethality included those deaths attributed to gunshot, hanging, falling under a vehicle, and electrocution. Lower lethality encompassed methods like poisoning, drug overdose, cuts, and suffocation. This classification scheme is similar to those used in past work (e.g., Card, 1974). Joiner's results showed that those individuals with greater lethality methods endorsed more burdensomeness in their notes than those with less lethal methods. Some studies have suggested that age appears to be a factor in degrees of burdensomeness. In a report by Foster (2003), individuals over the age of 65 who left notes were more likely to contain the theme of burden to others.

Among the suicide notes analyzed in one study, the majority (80%) stated a reason for the suicide (Bhatia et al., 2006), while the remaining 20% did not. Bhatia et al. found that from a study of 40 suicide notes (26 from males, 14 from females), different reasons were expressed for the decision to commit suicide, such as a disturbed love affair (25%), financial problems (15%), family disputes (10%), property disputes (10%), physical illness (10%), adultery (5%), and problems at work (5%). Kuwabara et al. (2006) presented six subgroups of reasons for suicide as reported in their notes, including: physical illness, pessimism, psychiatric disorder, problems in relationships, socioeconomic problems, and along with other reasons.

Lester et al. (2004) examined 262 suicide notes and incorporated Menninger's three motivations[2] for suicide to include to die, to kill, and to be killed and two additional factors (work/school and love/romance). Lester et al. found that older people who died by suicide were more likely to endorse the "to die" motive and less likely to have the "to kill" motive in their notes. The older group was also likely to use suicide to escape as a motive and less likely to have anger toward others as a motive. This finding was supported by a study which reported that the older group in the sample expressed less inwardly directed aggression in their suicide notes than the younger group (Leenaars & Balance, 1984).

Ho et al. (1998) indicated that the majority of individuals leaving a note provided practical instructions or directions regarding the handling of their affairs. The authors indicated that note leavers needed to communicate or disseminate specific information to others. In addition, the writer's age was related to whether the

[2] Menninger's three motives for suicide included expressions of anger (to kill), self-blame (to be killed), and the desire to escape (to die) (Lester, Seiden, & Tauber, 1990)

individuals addressed someone specific in their notes, with younger individuals more likely to write to parents, siblings, and friends and older individuals more likely to address spouses and children. Bhatia et al. (2006) reported that 35% of the sample did not address their suicide note to anyone, 20% of the subjects addressed their suicide note to a sibling, 15% to the police, 10% to a spouse or friend, and 5% to a parent or colleague.

Ho et al. (1998) theorized that an individual's religious beliefs might influence his/her need to write a note. Such individuals also tend to lack prior suicidal behaviors and often beg their readers to forgive them for committing suicide. Ho et al. wrote that, "In their last writings, suicide subjects reveal their remaining wishes and concerns, sometimes colored by their intense emotions" (p. 472).

Among the suicide notes in a study by Bhatia et al. (2006), over half of the sample indicated hopelessness and depression, 25% reported anguish and hostility, and 5% indicated signs of delusions. There was no clear indication that any of the individuals who died by suicide had a clear psychiatric illness (Bhatia et al.). In 80% of the suicide notes, death was reportedly the only option from the individuals' perspective.

c. Child Sex Offender Dynamics

CSOs often engage in a variety of behaviors to satisfy their sexual arousal to children. They may sexually molest children, produce sexually explicit images of children, download images of child pornography, distribute images of child pornography, and/or travel to have sex with a child. There is a diverse range in the intensity, frequency, time, effort, and motive for a person who sexually victimizes or exploits children. The FBI's BAU has been analyzing the behavior of CSOs for over 30 years and has developed the sex offender continuum, which has been instrumental in assisting law enforcement in understanding the sex offenders law enforcement investigates (Lanning, 2010). Two descriptive categories emerged within this continuum to provide a better understanding of the differences among this population. The continuum includes the situational CSO and the preferential CSO. A situational CSO is one who tends to be more opportunistic and impulsive in his sexual offending against children. This offender does not have an inherent sexual preference for children, but will take advantage of an opportunity to access children for a sexual purpose. Some studies have found that the situational CSO prefers adult partners, starts offending later on in life, has fewer victims, offends when stressed, and often offends against family members (Abel, Mittleman, & Becker, 1985). Alternatively, a preferential CSO has a long-standing, inherent, sexual arousal to children and often starts earlier in his offending (Lanning). The preferential CSO may incorporate ritualistic and/or obsessive actions in his collection and maintenance of child pornography to fulfill his arousal.

The majority of individuals who have a true sexual preference for children meet the criteria for pedophilia diagnosis if the child's age is 13 years or younger

(Lanning, 2010; Seto, 2008). The term pedophilia comes from the Greek words, "philia" meaning love and "pedeiktos" meaning young children (Seto). "Pedophilia erotica" was a term coined by Krafft-Ebbing (1886) in his book *Psychopathia Sexualis*, which described individuals who commit a violation against children under the age of 14 years. In the twentieth century, the term was broadly used and accepted to describe individuals who have a sexual interest and preference in children. The Diagnostic and Statistical Manual (DSM) of mental disorders first introduced the term in 1952. The DSM IV-Revised criteria for pedophilia includes the sexual interest in prepubescent minors (13 years and younger) by individuals who have had fantasies, sexual urges, or behaviors causing significant distress or impairment in social, occupational, or other areas and which has continued for 6 months or more. Some individuals diagnosed with pedophilia may not have acted upon their arousal, and some may not be distressed by their fantasies and urges. Acting on their arousal includes a broad list of behaviors and can include annoyance sex crimes with children such as exposure, voyeurism, frotteurism, and collecting child pornography. The diagnosis includes exclusive or nonexclusive types of pedophiles. The exclusive (sometimes referred to as a "true pedophile") type is only sexually interested in and aroused by children, while the nonexclusive type has a sexual interest in children and adults. In a study of 2,429 adult male pedophiles, only 7% self-identified as an exclusive type (Hall & Hall, 2007). Hence, most pedophiles fall into the nonexclusive category.

Additional changes are planned for the DSM-5, which is scheduled to be released in 2013 (www.dsm5.org) and includes revisions to the criteria and labels for the diagnosis of pedophilia. An additional category, "Pedohebephilic Disorder," is being proposed and would include prepubescent and pubescent children.

An accurate prevalence rate for pedophilia is difficult to obtain because an individual is typically identified by the legal system only after he acts on his sexual arousal to children. From an analysis of the studies to date, the best prevalence rate for individuals who meet the criteria for pedophilia among the male population is less than 5% with some studies ranging from 3% to 9% (Ahlers et al., 2009; Seto, 2008).

Finkelhor (1984) reported that individuals who meet the criteria for pedophilia have been found to have certain personality characteristics, such as low self-esteem and poor social skills, along with impaired interpersonal functioning (Cohen et al., 2002). Wilson and Cox (1983) reported that a sample of pedophiles showed elevations in the three factors of the three-factor model by Eysenck (1991) including psychoticism, introversion (extraversion), and neuroticism. A limitation of the research includes issues related to sampling. Most of the studies have focused on pedophiles who are in a correctional setting or in a clinical setting, and therefore, the results might be skewed.

CSOs act upon their sexual urges through online and contact offenses involving children. A question often asked of researchers studying CSOs is what likelihood exists that an online CSO has committed a sexual contact offense against a child (criminal history) or will engage in a sexual contact with a child in the future (recidivism)? There are limited empirical data to answer that question. A study by Bourke and Hernandez (2009), at the Bureau of Prisons, examined 155 online CSOs who were in a treatment program utilizing cognitive and behavioral treatment modalities.

The majority of the sample was Caucasian, and 74% had no known prior contact sexual offenses against children. When the polygraph was used in the treatment of the offenders, 85% admitted to having past contact sexual offenses against children and often had multiple victims. Although there are some limitations due to the fact that the sample is composed only of offenders who volunteered for treatment, this sample indicates that online CSOs were likely to have had a prior contact sexual offense against a child. Seto (2008) found that approximately 55% of a sample of pedophiles self-reported a prior sexual offense against a child and 12.5% had a documented prior contact sexual offense. In an unpublished study of online CSOs conducted by the FBI's BAU, approximately 33% had a prior history of or a subsequent contact child sexual offense. Of those who had a prior criminal history, 26.8% had been charged with a felony sex crime against a child. In addition, recidivism data was known for 189 online CSOs in the BAU sample. Of those offenders, the recidivism rate was 32% (n=61/189) with an average risk in the community of 4.4 years (SD=3.90 years) (FBI, 2010).

There are a number of factors impacting a CSO's decision to sexually offend against children. Seto (2008) reported that individuals who commit a hands-on offense against a child and are diagnosed with pedophilia offended against more victims. Eighty-eight percent of child molesters in the Seto sample met the criteria for pedophilia, and they committed most (95%) of the child abuse incidents. Factors influencing sexually offending against children can be organized by three main groups: (1) antisocial attitudes and behaviors, (2) sexual deviance, and (3) intimacy deficits (Finkelhor, 1984; Hall & Hirschman, 1992; Hanson & Morton-Bourgon, 2009; Seto, 2008; Ward & Beech, 2005). The antisocial category included those sex offenders who had a criminal history, a history of prior treatment for a sex offense, and a disinhibition due to alcohol, drug use, impulsivity, antisocial attitudes, and psychopathy. In addition, offenders who acted on their sexual arousal to children were able to overcome internal and external inhibitors and the child's resistance. The antisocial category also included cognitive distortions, which are used to justify sexual contact with children. Some CSOs also communicated with like-minded individuals, which reinforced their antisocial attitudes and beliefs. Finally, failing to comply with the requirements of their conditional release negatively impacts recidivism.

Another factor that impacts recidivism among CSOs is sexual deviance (Finkelhor, 1984; Hall & Hirschman, 1992; Seto, Hanson, & Babchishin, 2011). The following behaviors help to support and reinforce their physiological or deviant sexual arousal to children: possessing sexual material depicting younger children, sexual sadism, and possession of non-Internet child pornography. Research suggests that individuals who are strongly motivated by their sexual arousal to children would be considered preferential child sex offenders against children. Preferential CSOs typically have more victims due to their long-standing pattern of sexual interest and arousal to children. They often use less force as they are able to utilize well-developed grooming behaviors (Hall & Hirschman; Lanning, 2010).

The third factor, intimacy deficits, includes being unable to meet sexual and intimacy needs from adults, being more connected emotionally to children, having poor social skills, having affective dysregulation, being single, having prior male child victims, and loneliness. CSOs with affect-related problems (affective dysregulation) are often opportunistic in their victim choices, use greater violence, and commit both sexual and nonsexual offenses (Hall & Hirschman, 1992).

Additionally, having a personality disorder impacts the antisocial attitudes and behaviors, sexual deviance, and intimacy deficits of CSOs. People who have personality-disordered traits often have a greater vulnerability, which increases affective dysregulation, impulsivity, sexual arousal, and thoughts about children.

The preferential CSO or pedophile who acts upon his sexual arousal to children utilizes varied methods to obtain his preferred child victim, including accessing the child through his neighborhood, employment choices or hobbies, marrying a woman who has children, marrying in order to have children, and meeting other like-minded individuals who may have access to children and who can support and condone such behavior (Lanning, 2010). He employs well-developed strategies to seduce and groom children for sexual purposes. The goal of grooming is to slowly build the child's trust in order to reduce the risk of exposure and/or disclosure, to gain access to the child through the parents, to obtain time alone to develop this trust, and to desensitize the child to eventually engage in sexual contact with the offender (Lanning).

The grooming techniques used depend on the age and specific needs or vulnerabilities of the child and may include giving the child gifts; support; treating the child as special; isolating the victim from his/her social support; gradually increasing the explicit talk about sex through jokes, education, use of pornography (adult and/or child); and gradually desensitizing the child to touch (e.g., tickling, wrestling, bathing) (Lanning, 2010).

In order to fully examine CSO dynamics, one must understand the internal conflict often experienced by offenders during their offending (Hoffer, Shelton, Behnke, & Erdberg, 2010). This internal conflict is often overcome by using cognitive distortions, which help an offender maintain a positive sense of self and suppress feelings of shame or anxiety. There is substantial literature exploring the cognitive, emotional, and behavioral deficits that CSOs exhibit and the relationship between cognitive distortions and child sexual abuse (Abel et al., 1989; Howitt & Sheldon 2007; Lanning, 2010; Murphy, 1990; Seto, 2008).

Cognitive distortions, such as denial, rationalization, and minimization, allow CSOs to misconstrue the nature of their sexual offending and defend against the full impact of their sexual arousal to children (Abel et al., 1989; Lanning, 2010; Murphy, 1990; Ward, 2000). Using these distortions allows the offender to excuse his behavior to himself and others (Howitt, 2005; Howitt & Sheldon 2007; Lanning). Examples of these distortions include, "I only looked at pictures of child pornography," or "I am addicted to pornography," "I'm not interested in child pornography," "I love children and would never hurt them," "that little girl came onto me by sitting on my lap," or "the child pornography just popped up on my computer, and I was just curious." Yet, when law enforcement knocks on the CSO's door, his secret is exposed, and the cognitive distortions he has used for so many years may no longer effectively protect him from feelings of self-loathing (Hoffer et al., 2010).

Based on an extensive review of studies, Ward (2000) established categories of cognitive distortions generated by CSOs. They include the following: (1) the offender believes the child desires and needs sexual pleasure and can make an informed decision about sexual contact; (2) the CSO thinks he is entitled and his needs are more important than others; (3) the offender views the world as a dangerous place, and children are more trustworthy and safer than adults; (4) the offender believes that his behavior is out of his control, and other factors (e.g., alcohol, drugs) are responsible for his sexual behavior; (5) the offender perceives that the sexual activity with children is basically harmless compared with more severe behaviors.

d. Child Sex Offenders and Suicide

In exploring suicide among CSOs, only a few studies have specifically addressed the topic with earlier work consisting primarily of case studies rather than empirical analyses (Walford, Kennedy, Manwell, & McCune, 1990; Wild, 1998). Even among historical and more recent studies, trends and patterns have been observed and noted.

Brophy (2003) studied 32 subjects who committed suicide while under investigation for a sexual offense. Sexual offenses included offenses against adults or children; however, sexual offenses committed against children comprised the majority of the study. Findings revealed a sample of all males, on average in their mid-40s, whose deaths typically occurred very early in the criminal investigation. Nearly half were married and most died by hanging. None of the 32 men had a prior sex offense, and many were in good standing in their community. When comparing suicide risk with the general population of Irish males, the sex offenders who offended against children were 230 times more likely to commit suicide. Brophy found that the offender's shame and "catastrophic loss of standing and irreparable damage to [his] reputation" are most closely linked to the offender's subsequent suicide (p. 158). He attributes that shame affects these offenders more than despair. Biological influences also may be at play with CSOs under investigation as highlighted by Buck (1999) who found that decreasing blood serotonin levels (linked to impulsive aggression and suicide) followed a change in social standing (Brophy, 2003). Additionally, Brophy reported that offenders exhibit elevated stress and an increased risk of self-harm at *each* step of the legal process instead of at one particular stage due to the anticipation regarding future outcomes. For those CSOs who cope with the stress, the result is an acceptance and adjustment to each legal phase (e.g., awareness, arrest, detention, release, indictment, preliminary hearing, trial, plea, sentencing, incarceration). For CSOs who are not able to cope effectively with the elevated stress, the potential for self-harm increases.

Pritchard and King (2005) also found similar risk patterns and differentiated types of child sex offenders. Examining 16 suicides among 374 male CSOs, they divided the sample into three groups: (1) sex only (51%), those offenders whose only criminal offense was a child sex crime; (2) multi-criminal (27%), offenders whose offenses included a child sex crime as well as other nonsexual crimes; and (3) violent multi-criminal (22%), offenders whose criminal offenses included a child sex crime, along with other nonsexual crimes, and at least one conviction for violence (Pritchard & Bagley, 2000).[1] Analyses revealed that 15 of the 16 suicides occurred among offenders whose only criminal offense was a child sex crime. Offenders in this group, who most often killed themselves around the time of the disclosure of the sex crime or trial, were 183 times more likely to die by suicide than the male general population. Pritchard and King (2005) discussed a variety of factors to explain why CSOs with no prior criminal offenses are at higher risk for suicide. These included shame or remorse, media exposure, threat and pressure of criminal proceedings, and future prison time (Prichard & King, 2005).

Byrne, Lurigio, and Pimentel (2009) also highlight the need to study CSO suicide in order to reformulate suicide prevention policies and practices. This study examined suicides among alleged sex offenders in the federal pretrial system and what appears to be a significantly high risk of suicide in these defendants. Although extensive research has been conducted of prison/jail suicides, suicide among those on community supervision (pretrial, probation, parole) is lacking (Pritchard & King, 2005). Therefore, in response to the fast-growing number of federally prosecuted child exploitation offenses, and the number of suicides of pretrial sex offenders in two California federal districts, a pilot program was established to attempt to lower the risk of suicide in this population. The program allows for a multidisciplinary approach with mental health providers and the criminal justice system working together in crisis intervention, therapy, and incarceration preparations (Byrne et al., 2009). Since the program's inception, no suicides have occurred among participants. The researchers hope that it sets the example of how new and innovative strategies can prevent suicide among this population of offenders.

A more recent article explored the issues and widespread impact surrounding CSOs who commit suicide and underscores the potential risk to law enforcement personnel (Hoffer et al., 2010). Increased awareness by law enforcement of the potential for suicide in child sex crime investigations may mitigate the risk of suicide and improve operational responses, including officer safety. The article not only detailed how the offender is impacted by the investigation but also addressed how the offender's subsequent suicide affects his family, friends, and victims.

Because many CSOs experience high levels of fear, anxiety, shame, and helplessness after learning they are under investigation, suicide may be viewed as the preferred alternative when they consider the loss of their job, home, reputation, and freedom. Upon their death, their family suffers tremendous loss, which is compounded by the discovery that a loved one has committed sexual crimes against children. Family members may experience feelings of guilt, anger, denial, and shock, and may be left wondering if they ever really even knew their loved one at all. Quite similarly, victim(s) of the offender often experience a range of feelings after the suicide to include ambivalence, anger, and sadness. Depending on the type of relationship between the offender and victim, others may blame the victim for

[1] Violent offenses were defined as nonsexual offenses with actual or grievous bodily harm (Prichard & Bagley, 2000).

causing the offender's death due to his/her disclosure of sexual molestation, thus increasing the victim's distress, guilt, and inner turmoil (Hoffer et al., 2010).

In addition to exploring the impact of CSO suicide on family members, victims of the CSO, and law enforcement, the purpose of this study was to examine the risk indicators for suicide, along with behavioral and personality factors of the CSOs who died by suicide by obtaining information from the investigation, lead investigators, along with family members and close associations of the CSO. In addition, the analyses of the suicide notes offered insight into the cognitive and affective state of the CSO. The results of the study impact multidisciplinary fields to include law enforcement, legal, mental health, and corrections.

III. Method

Inclusion criteria requirements for the study were the following: (1) The offender was under investigation for a child sex crime at the time of his death, (2) the offender was aware that he was being investigated,[1] and (3) the offender's death was officially ruled a suicide or involved a suicide-by-cop scenario, as determined by a coroner, medical examiner, or through investigative records. A child sex crime was defined as receiving, possessing, distributing, or producing child pornography, traveling to have sex with a minor, or sexually molesting a child(ren). One hundred and six active investigations between 1998 and 2010 were examined in this study. Cases were primarily identified through the FBI's internal Automated Case Support (ACS) database with additional cases provided by local and state law enforcement agencies. Cases represented 39 FBI field offices and 32 states. The method of identifying subjects included using query terms such as "suicide," "death," "killed," and "self-harm."

a. Materials and Procedure

Upon identifying offenders who met the inclusion criteria, trained researchers assigned to the Crimes Against Children section of the FBI's BAU reviewed case records related to each investigation. Death investigation reports and autopsy reports were also requested and reviewed. Thereafter, follow-up calls were made to the case agent/detective in order to obtain additional information that could not be discerned from the case materials.

Initially, the study focused on the review of law enforcement investigative materials and the interviews with the lead investigators on each case. After coding 106

[1] The criteria for inclusion into the study were cases at each investigative process, such as following a knock and talk, search warrant, prior to or following an arrest warrant, a plea agreement, a trial, conviction, sentencing, or incarceration.

T.A. Hoffer and J.L.E. Shelton, *Suicide Among Child Sex Offenders*,
SpringerBriefs in Psychology, DOI 10.1007/978-1-4614-5937-8_3,
© Springer Science+Business Media New York 2013

cases, the researchers began an additional data gathering procedure, which entailed interviewing family members and/or close associates and administering the general assessment questionnaire[2] (GAQ), a questionnaire about the subject to obtain background and personality characteristics.

i. *General Assessment Questionnaire*

The GAQ was developed approximately 20 years ago by the FBI's BAU to obtain information regarding an individual's background and personality characteristics based on the five-factor model of personality. The questionnaire is a paper-pencil written document which contains 119 questions related to an individual's family history, education, employment history, past substance or alcohol issues, abuse history, hobbies, interests, sexual history, etc. The GAQ provides a broad-based assessment of information relative to an individual's interpersonal style, coping abilities, needs and motives, his/her character, levels of emotional well-being, and other psychological characteristics that can better help understand the individual's strengths and weaknesses (Piedmont, 1998).

In addition, the GAQ includes an adjective scale which captures personality characteristics based on a well-established personality theory. Over many years, personality characteristics have been organized in order to capture personality constructs, encompassing three to 16 factors (Eysenck, 1991; Cattell, Cattell, & Cattell, 2000). Hans Eysenck introduced a three-factor model of personality including psychoticism, extraversion, and neuroticism, which is related to the five-factor model (FFM) of personality (Eysenck).

The FFM, commonly referred to as the big five, includes openness, conscientiousness, extraversion, agreeableness, and neuroticism (OCEAN) (Costa & McCrae, 1992). Individuals who are rated as high on the openness factor are more creative and innovative compared to those who score low and tend to be closed minded and conservative. High conscientiousness indicates individuals who are careful, deliberate, organized, and dutiful, while those who are low on conscientiousness tend to be sloppy, impulsive, and disorganized. Those high on extraversion are outgoing individuals who prefer to be social versus low on extraversion (introversion), which describes those who are less socially motivated. Agreeableness indicates how individuals view their world and get along with others. High agreeableness indicates they are cooperative, altruistic, and trustworthy, while low agreeableness indicates they are more callous, inflexible, and devious in their interactions with others. The last factor, neuroticism, captures the ability of individuals to adjust and to cope with stressors or distressing situations in their lives. Neuroticism indicates the individuals' locus of control or how much they attribute events in their

[2]The FBI's BAU-III has examined the reliability and validity of the assessment questionnaire.

lives as happening to them versus having control over events in their world. Individuals high on neuroticism are overly sensitive, fragile, with increased emotional instability in their world. Low neuroticism indicates individuals who are calm, stable, and easygoing (Costa & McCrae).

Psychological assessments have been developed to capture the cognitive, emotional, and behavioral functioning of individuals (Cattell et al., 2000; Costa & McCrae, 1992; Eysenck, 1991) and their various personality factors through both a direct and indirect assessment process. The direct psychological evaluation can include tests such as the Minnesota Multiphasic Psychological Inventory – 2 (Butcher & Megargee, 2001), the Millon Clinical Multiaxial Inventory – III Third Edition, (MCMI-III Millon, Davis, Millon, & Grossman, 2009), and the 16 PF (Personality Factors) (Cattell et al.). Though less prevalent, there are assessment tools that allow for an indirect assessment of the individual, such as the Neuroticism, Extraversion, Openness Personality Inventory Revised (NEO-PI-R), by Costa and McCrae.

The NEO-PI-R was specifically developed to capture the FFM and is a widely utilized and reliable inventory that measures genotypic and phenotypic qualities of normal personality (Rossier, de Stadelhofen, & Berthoud, 2004) through domain and facet scales. For example, the domain of extraversion represents a genotypic quality, while a facet of extraversion, such as gregariousness, represents the phenotypic expression of extraversion. This phenotypic expression will typically change over time, but the underlying genotype will remain fairly constant, particularly past the age of 30 (Costa & McCrae, 1992; Piedmont, 1998) (Table 1).

The GAQ incorporated the FFM due to the significant research conducted on this model of personality. The GAQ was chosen for its utility in enabling an indirect interview with individuals who knew the subject well and could provide the researchers with pertinent data on the subject for the study. The advantages of the GAQ include (1) the shorter length of the instrument, (2) the use of the observer-report forms, (3) the use of observer-report forms to capture traits of a deceased individual, and (4) a digital scoring format for analysis. In addition, the GAQ does not require the interviewer to have any specified psychological training in order to administer the instrument.

The instrument has been validated and the GAQ adjectives are consistent with the FFM domains scales of openness, conscientiousness, extraversion, agreeableness, and neuroticism (Yates, 2012).

Researchers were unable to interview a family and/or close associate for every subject either due to an unwillingness to participate, the lack of current contact information for associates, or time constraints. Sixteen interviews of subjects' family members or close associates have been conducted and family members or close associates have completed 31 GAQs to date.

Data collected from case records and interviews were extracted and recorded onto a 150-question protocol that was developed by the BAU and peer reviewed by the BAU's Behavioral Research Working Group (BRWG). The BRWG, composed of 17 nationally and internationally recognized researchers, scholars, and practitioners, assists the BAU in producing high quality, academically sound research.

Table 1 Domain and facet scales of the NEO-PI-R

Neuroticism (*N*)	Extraversion (*E*)	Openness to experience (*O*)	Agreeableness (*A*)	Conscientiousness (*C*)
N1 Anxiety	*E1* Warmth	*O1* Fantasy	*A1* Trust	*C1* Competence
N2 Angry hostility	*E2* Gregariousness	*O2* Aesthetics	*A2* Straightforwardness	*C2* Order
N3 Depression	*E3* Assertiveness	*O3* Feelings	*A3* Altruism	*C3* Dutifulness
N4 Self-consciousness	*E4* Activity	*O4* Actions	*A4* Compliance	*C4* Achievement striving
N5 Impulsiveness	*E5* Excitement-seeking	*O5* Ideas	*A5* Modesty	*C5* Self-discipline
N6 Vulnerability	*E6* Positive emotions	*O6* Values	*A6* Tender mindedness	*C6* Deliberation

Note. Adapted from Miller, Reynolds, and Pilkonis (2004)

The protocol is divided into three main areas: offender background, sex crime investigation details, and suicide information. Offender background information includes demographics, as well as educational, marital, employment, medical, mental health (to include suicidal behavior), abuse/maltreatment, and criminal histories. The sex crime investigation section includes questions such as the type of sex crime, date, location of the offense, contact offense victim demographics (age, gender, relationship to the offender, access), child pornography collection descriptions, computer activities, and how the offender became aware of the investigation. In addition, prosecutive information is captured in order to determine at what point in the legal process the suicide occurred. The suicide information section includes questions about the date, location, method, cause of death, substance use, and the presence of a suicide note(s).

ii. Suicide Notes

The suicide notes of the CSOs were coded based upon a protocol that was developed by the FBI's BAU. The suicide note analysis protocol includes a number of factors, including cognitive distortions (denial, minimization, rationalization). Denial was defined as "unpleasant thoughts, feelings, wishes or events that are ignored or excluded from conscious awareness in order to resolve emotional conflict and reduce anxiety" (VandenBos, 2006, p. 268). Minimization was defined as a "tendency to present events to oneself or others as insignificant or unimportant. It often involves being unclear and nonspecific, leading to inaccurate or incomplete conclusion" (VandenBos, p. 582). Rationalization was defined as "an explanation in which apparent logical reasons are given to justify an unacceptable behavior" (VandenBos, p. 770).

Other factors incorporated into the protocol included self-blame, other blame, apology, addressee, practical information, detached tone, expressions of love and affection, discussion of life after death, details regarding suicide act, specifics regarding the investigation or legal process, shame, the five-factor model (FFM) (openness, conscientiousness, extraversion, agreeableness, neuroticism), and the interpersonal–psychological theory model (Joiner, 2005). In addition, coders captured various aspects represented in the notes and included consideration of others/sparing of the feelings of others, clear/direct anger; low self-esteem, grief stricken, feeling defeated/overwhelmed, unable to show feelings, medical illness, performance failure, feeling sorry for oneself, difficulty coping, obtaining forgiveness, taking control, depression, narcissistic/self-absorbed tone, impression management, pessimism, detachment from self or others, fear/anxiety, ambivalence, and/or selfishness about the suicide act. Finally, if noted, the following reasons for suicide were captured: physical illness, emotional/mental problems, problems with relationship, failures, CSO investigation, anger at others, anger at self, escape from his unbearable pain, and to take control. Coding the CSO's reasons for the suicide was based on direct statements along with the totality of statements in the letter including vague, generalized, or implied explanations, which resulted in an element of subjectivity.

Interrater reliability was established by initially having three coders review the same case. Each coder completed a protocol and any discrepancies were discussed and resolved. During the coding of the remaining cases, any conflicting questions were reviewed by the primary coder. Descriptive and frequency statistics were generated using IBM SPSS Version 19.0 (SPSS, Chicago, IL).

IV. Results

a. Offender Characteristics

i. Gender, Age, and Race

The gender of the 106 offenders was entirely male. The average age was 48 years (SD = 11.3, range 24–71). Fourteen percent (n = 15) of the offenders were between 24 and 34 years of age, 27% (n = 29) were 35–44 years of age, 25% (n = 27) were 45–54 years of age, and 33% (n = 35) were 55 years of age or older. Ninety-seven percent (n = 103) of offenders were Caucasian, 1% (n = 1) were African-American, 1% (n = 1) were Hispanic, and 1% (n = 1) offender were considered other race (Middle Eastern).

ii. Marital Status

The offender's marital status at time of the suicide was known for 104 of the 106 offenders (98%). Fifty-five percent (n = 57) of offenders were not married, while 45% (n = 47) were married. Of the 55% of offenders who were not married, marital/relationship history was known for 49 offenders: 53% (n = 26) had never been married, 35% (n = 17) offenders were divorced, 8% (n = 4) were cohabitating with an intimate partner, and 4% (n = 2) were widowed.

iii. Children

Whether the offender had children at the time of his death was known in 104 of the 106 cases (98%). Sixty percent (n = 62) of the offenders had children, while 40%

T.A. Hoffer and J.L.E. Shelton, *Suicide Among Child Sex Offenders*,
SpringerBriefs in Psychology, DOI 10.1007/978-1-4614-5937-8_4,
© Springer Science+Business Media New York 2013

(n=42) did not. Ninety percent (n=56) of the children were biological children; 21% (n=13) were stepchildren; 5% (n=3) were adopted children; and 2% (n=1) were foster children.

When available, the ages of the offender's children were captured in two categories: minor (less than 18 years of age) or adult (18 years of age or older). For 56 of the 62 offenders with children (90%), this information was known. Of the 56 offenders, 23 (41%) had children under the age of 18 at the time of their deaths, 30 (54%) had adult children, and 3 (5%) offenders had both minor and adult children.

iv. Education Level

The offender's education level was known in 71 of the 106 cases (67%). Of the known cases, 37 (52%) had received a college degree, and 12 (17%) offenders had attended some college. Fifteen (21%) offenders graduated from high school, and four (6%) offenders received some high school education. Two (3%) attended a tech/trade school, and one (1%) received his general equivalency diploma (GED).

Of those 37 offenders who had received a college degree, degree type was known in 28 cases (76%). Of the 28 known cases, 12 (43%) obtained bachelor's level degrees, seven (25%) received master's degrees, five (18%) earned their Ph.D., two (7%) obtained law degrees, and two (7%) received associate degrees.

v. Employment Status

The offender's employment status at the time of the suicide was known for 97 of the 106 offenders (92%). Of the 97 known cases, 62% (n=60) of offenders were employed, 25% (n=24) were unemployed, and 13% (n=13) were coded as other (retired, disabled, administrative leave). In 23% (n=19) of the cases, there were recent employment disciplinary actions against the offender due to the investigation; these most often involved being fired, asked to leave, or forced to resign from their jobs.

vi. Military History

The military history of the offender was known in 78 of the 106 cases (74%). Of the 78 known cases, 35 (45%) offenders had served in the United States Armed Forces. Eight (22%) offenders served in the Army and Navy, respectively, followed by seven in the Marine Corp (19%), Air Force (n=4, 11%), Coast Guard (n=1, 3%), and National Guard (n=1, 3%). For six (19%) offenders, the armed forces branch was unknown. Overall, 34 (97%) offenders had past service experience, and one offender (3%) was on active duty at the time of his suicide.

vii. Criminal Arrest History

The FBI's Criminal Justice Information System (CJIS) performed a criminal history record check on all 106 offenders. For 11 offenders, their criminal history is unknown because there were no identifiable results within the database.

The results were coded using the National Incident Based Reporting System (NIBRS). Of the 95 offenders who were identifiable in the database, 44% (n=42) had a criminal arrest history prior to the investigation; collectively, they were charged with 84 offenses. The number of offenses per offender ranged from one to six, with over half (52%) being arrested for one offense. Offenses included other (n=14) (i.e., conspiracy to commit larceny, contempt, obstructing a peace officer, driving on suspended license, failure to appear, probation violation, fugitive, harassment, immigration violation, indecent exposure, tax evasion, offensive words), forcible sex offense (n=12), driving under the influence (n=10), larceny/theft (n=7), assault (n=7), drug/narcotics (n=5), burglary/breaking and entering (n=4), fraud (n=4), bad checks (n=3), pornography/obscene material (n=3), destruction/damage/vandalism to property (n=3), trespassing (n=2), kidnapping/abduction (n=2), counterfeit/forgery (n=1), embezzlement (n=1), prostitution (n=1), stolen property (n=1), weapon violation (n=1), family nonviolent offense (n=1), disorderly conduct (n=1), and peeping tom (n=1).

b. Investigation Characteristics

i. Offender Types

Each offender was classified into categories based on the type of child sex crime(s) he committed. Classification of each offender was based on reviews of investigative reports, criminal history, and statements by the offender and his family members and/or close associates. The four categories were (1) *trader*, a person who trafficked in and collected child pornography; (2) *molester*, a person involved in hands-on sexual contact with a child; (3) *traveler*, a person who traveled (usually interstate) to have sex with an actual child he communicated with online or an undercover law enforcement officer who posed as a child; and (4) *producer*, a person who created child pornography. These categories were not mutually exclusive, and offenders could be placed into more than one category.

Seventy-nine percent (n=84) of the offenders were classified as traders, followed by 43% (n=45) as molesters, 21% (n=22) as travelers, and 18% (n=19) as producers. Forty-three percent (n=46) of the offenders were classified in more than one category.

ii. *Demographics of Hands-On/Contact Child Victims*

The 45 identified molesters offended against a total of 109 children. The gender was known for 102 of 109 child victims (94%). Sixty-five percent (n=66) of the victims were female, and 35% (n=36) were male. The victim's race/ethnicity was known for 75 of the 109 victims (69%). The overwhelming majority (91%) of the victims were Caucasian (n=68), followed by 5% (n=4) Asian, 3% (n=2) African-American, and 1% (n=1) Hispanic. Victim age was captured in three categories: (a) 5 years of age or younger, (b) 6–12 years of age, and (c) 13–17 years of age. In some cases, victims were placed in more than one age category if the molestation occurred for an extended period of time. Victim age was known for 81 of the 109 victims (74%). Ten percent (n=8) of the victims were 5 years of age or younger. Fifty-three percent (n=43) of the victims were 6–12 years of age, and 47% (n=38) were 13–17 years of age. Relationship between the offender and the victim was captured in two categories, familial or nonfamilial. This relationship was known for 104 of the 109 victims (95%). For 61% (n=63) of the victims, the relationship between the victim and the offender was nonfamilial. For 39% (n=41) of the victims, the relationship was familial. The types of sex acts perpetrated by the offender were fondling (n=60, 74%), oral sex (n=40, 49%), masturbation (n=25, 31%), vaginal sex (n=19, 24%), other sex act (n=12, 15%), digital penetration (n=7, 9%), anal sex (n=6, 7%), and foreign object insertion (n=5, 6%).

iii. *Awareness of Investigation*

Fifty percent (n=53) of offenders became aware of the investigation when law enforcement executed a search warrant at his residence and/or place of work. Thirty-two percent (n=33) of offenders became aware of the investigation during a "knock and talk" interview with law enforcement. In 14% (n=15) of the cases, the offender learned of the investigation via an arrest warrant, and in 4% (n=4) of cases, the offender became aware of the investigation from a third party (e.g., family member, friend, and media). One (1%) case was classified as "other" because the offender killed himself after abducting the victim, knowing law enforcement was looking for him.

c. Suicide Characteristics

i. *Stressors*

A variety of stressors was present for each offender around the time of the suicide. All offenders experienced at least one stressor, and collectively, there were 224 responses in the stressor categories. Most common were criminal/legal problems from the investigation (N=106, 100%), followed by physical injury/illness (n=41, 39%), marital problems (n=18, 17%), job-related stress (n=24, 23%), other (n=14, 13%), financial strain (n=10, 9%), mental health problems (n=5, 5%), recent change in family dynamics (n=3, 3%), and death of relative/friend (n=2, 2%).

ii. Household Composition

The offender's household composition at the time of the suicide was known in 95 of the 106 cases (90%). Of the known cases, 39 (41%) offenders lived alone. Fifty-six (59%) offenders lived with someone else including spouse (n=34, 61%), children (n=23, 41%), parents (n=9, 16%), friends (n=5, 9%), significant other (n=5, 9%), siblings (n=1, 2%), other relative (n=1, 2%), and other (landlord) (n=1, 2%).

iii. Time Between Awareness and Suicide

Time between the offender's awareness of the investigation and suicide was divided into four categories: (a) within 48 hours, (b) within 30 days, (c) within 1 year, and (d) over 1 year. In 26% (n=28) of the cases, the offender's suicide occurred within 48 hours of his awareness of the investigation. Twenty-eight percent (n=30) of the offenders committed suicide within 30 days of awareness, followed by 26% (n=28) occurring within 1 year and 19% (n=20) occurring after 1 year from awareness. After combining the first two categories, the cumulative percent revealed that 55% (n=58) of the offenders committed suicide within the first month of their awareness of the investigation.

iv. Suicide and Investigative Stage

Four investigative stages were created for reporting when the suicide occurred: (a) investigative period, after awareness but before arrest; (b) judicial period, after arrest but before conviction; (c) incarceration period, after conviction and while serving a sentence; and (d) post-incarceration period, after serving a sentence.

Fifty-five percent (n=58) of offenders committed suicide during the investigative period, followed by 43% (n=46) during the judicial period. One offender committed suicide while incarcerated, and one committed suicide after incarceration.

v. Cause of Death (COD)

In 100 (94%) cases, a single COD was identified by the medical examiner or pathologist. Over half (52%) were the result of a gunshot wound, followed by hanging (n=23, 23%), drug overdose (n=8, 8%), carbon monoxide poisoning (n=8, 8%), blunt force trauma (from a jump/fall) (n=3, 3%), suffocation with plastic bag (n=2, 2%), drowning (n=2, 2%), cutting/stabbing (n=1, 1%), and huffing (n=1, 1%).

In six (6%) cases, the examining pathologist listed the COD as being multifactorial. Of the multifactorial COD cases, the following causes were reported: overdose (n=3), cutting/stabbing (n=3), carbon monoxide poisoning (n=3), suffocation with plastic bag (n=1), and drowning (n=1).

vi. Suicide Location

In 32% (n=34) of the cases, the offender committed suicide in a nonresidential outdoor location (e.g., road, field, bridge, park, woods). The suicide location was inside the offender's residence in 32% (n=34) of the cases, followed by prison/jail (n=12, 11%), external property of the offender's residence (n=10, 9%), hotel/motel room (n=8, 8%), business (n=4, 4%), and water (n=3, 3%). In one case, the offender killed himself in an unoccupied, abandoned trailer.

vii. Potential Danger to Law Enforcement

In 10% (n=11) of the cases, there was potential for harm to law enforcement at the time of the offender's suicide. The most common scenario was when the offender shot and killed himself while in the presence of, or in close proximity to, law enforcement officers. At the time of the suicide, law enforcement personnel were attempting to make contact with the offender for a variety of reasons including executing a search or arrest warrant, attempting a knock and talk, or after the offender failed to show for a court appearance.

d. Suicide Notes

The offender left a suicide note or other type of communication in 68% (n=72) of the cases. Notes were left in a variety of formats to include handwritten and typed letters, text messages, and videos. These communications were most commonly directed to the offender's spouse, girlfriend, children, and other family members. In some cases, the letters were addressed to emergency medical personnel and law enforcement.

Of the 72 CSOs who wrote a suicide note, the mean age was 46 years, and the median age was 44 years, with a range of 24–66 years. Fifty-four percent (n=39) of the CSOs were not married at the time of their deaths. Forty-six percent (n=33) of the CSOs were married. Sixty-three percent (n=45) had children, with 50% having adult children and 45% with minor children.

Fifty-two percent (n=26) were college graduates with an additional 18% (n=9) having attended some college. Of those with a college degree, 31% (n=8) obtained an advanced degree (e.g., masters, law, or Ph.D.). Fifty-nine percent (n=40) were employed at the time of their deaths, and 28% (n=19) were unemployed. Twenty-two percent (n=12) had recent disciplinary actions against them by their employer due to the investigation (e.g., administrative leave or retirement – asked or forced). Forty-three percent (n=23) were known to have current or past military service. Forty-seven percent (n=30) had a prior criminal history.

Forty-two percent (n=30) had recent significant medical problems/history at the time of their deaths. Twenty-four percent (n=17) died by suicide within 48 hours of becoming aware of the investigation. Thirty-one percent (n=22) died by suicide within 30 days, 25% (n=18) within 1 year, and 21% (n=15) over 1 year.

Fifty-three percent (n=38) lived with someone else, while 38% (n=27) lived alone. Six percent (n=4) were living in a jail cell at the time of their deaths. Forty-seven percent (n=34) died by self-inflicted gunshot wound.

Of the 72 offenders who left a suicide note, the researchers were able to obtain a copy of the note in 81% (n=58) of the cases. The offender specifically addressed the note to a particular individual or group of individuals in 85% (n=49) of the notes analyzed. For 74% (n=43) of the cases, the offender provided practical instructions and/or information in the note. Sixty-nine percent (n=40) discussed the criminal investigation against them in their note. For many of the offenders, the investigation was not directly discussed, but was often addressed using words like "consequences," "loss of freedom," "betrayed the trust of others," "all that is happening," "accusations," "screwed up big time," and "storm that is approaching."

i. Cognitive Distortions

The notes were analyzed for the presence of three cognitive distortions: (1) denial, (2) minimization, and (3) rationalization. Collectively, 66% (n=38) of the offenders had at least one cognitive distortion present in their note. Twenty-four percent (n=16) of the notes analyzed contained expressions of denial most often related to the investigation pending against them. Forty-two percent (n=28) of the notes contained expressions of minimization. Minimization was most commonly expressed in the form of addressing their sexual interest in children as a problem, lack of judgment, or mistake, and they emphasized that they never intentionally wanted to hurt anyone. Thirty-four percent (n=23) of the notes had statements of rationalizations, to include saying "demons," "monsters," and compulsions in their heads were the reason or excuse for their behavior. Rationalization was used not only when addressing the allegations against them but also when discussing why they chose to commit suicide.

ii. *Self-Blame and Blaming of Others*

In 78% (n=45) of the notes, the offender wrote statements of self-blame. Statements of self-blame most often consisted of generalized statements as opposed to directly addressing his responsibility for the accusations(s). Generalized statements frequently discussed how they had "messed up" their life, been a disappointment, and made a lot of mistakes. In 37% (n=21) of the notes, the offender blamed others. Blaming others most often included events (e.g., deaths of loved ones, divorce, difficult childhood) in the past or relationship problems with family members. In some cases, the offender held law enforcement responsible for ruining their lives.

iii. *Apology*

In 69% (n=40) of the notes, the offender specifically apologized to others for leaving them this way and/or causing pain and embarrassment in their lives.

iv. *Shame*

Fifty-nine percent (n=34) of the offenders expressed shame in their notes by describing their lives as being dishonorable to themselves and others. In almost all cases, the expressions of shame were indirect and generalized to their entire lives as opposed to the acts they were accused of committing.

v. *Discussion of Afterlife*

Seventy-four percent (n=42) of the offenders' notes did not contain statements about life after death. In 26% (n=15), the offenders did discuss an afterlife in a both negative and positive tone (e.g., "I've repented, and God will welcome me into his kingdom," or "I am banishing myself to an eternity in hell").

vi. *Suicide Act*

Twenty-one percent (n=12) of the offenders discussed specific details about the actual suicide act in their notes. Their statements varied, but often included discussions regarding the planning of their death and the suicide methods that they chose.

Table 2 Aspects and features of suicide notes

Aspect/feature	*n*	Freq. (%)
Consideration/sparing of feelings of others	32	55
Feeling sorry for oneself	26	45
Obtaining forgiveness (God, family)	24	41
Taking control	21	36
Feeling defeated/overwhelmed	16	28
Pessimism/pervasive negativity	15	26
Impression management	14	24
Difficulty coping	13	23
Depression	11	19
Low self-esteem	11	19
Subtle/indirect anger	9	16
Clear/direct anger	8	14
Narcissistic/self-absorbed tone	7	12
Ambivalence about suicide act	7	12
Grief stricken	6	10
Performance failure	6	10
Medical illness	4	7
Unable to show feelings	4	7
Selfishness about the suicide act ("This is selfish!")	3	5
Detached from self (fantasy based/eccentric elements)	3	5
Fear/anxiety about suicide act	2	3
Total*	242	417

Note. * Multi-response

vii. Elements of Joiner's Interpersonal-Psychological Theory (IPT)

Seventy-nine percent (n=46) of the notes had at least one element of the IPT. Fifty-four percent (n=41) contained expressions of burdensomeness. Thirty-one percent (n=23) contained elements of thwarted/lack of belonging, and 15% (n=11) had expressions which would increase one's acquired capability for suicide.

viii. Aspects and Features

Aspects and features were classified within the suicide notes. Table 2 displays the multiple responses that were coded.

ix. Reasons for Suicide

In 55 of the 58 (98%) notes, the offender discussed his reason(s) for committing suicide. Of the 55 cases, 62% (n=34) listed the CSO investigation as a reason for

Table 3 Elements of the five-factor model

Frequency of the five factors (*n*)						
	O	C	E	A	N	Total
High	18% (*8*)	55% (*24*)	7% (*3*)	7% (*3*)	55% (*24*)	141% (*62*)
Low	59% (*10*)	5% (*1*)	9% (2)	59% (*13*)	0% (*0*)	118% (*26*)

Note. Percentages are based on the total of known responses. Components of the FFM are presented above: *O* openness, *C* conscientiousness, *E* extraversion, *A* agreeableness, *N* neuroticism. Adapted from Costa and McCrae (1992)

their suicide. In 55% (n = 30), the reason listed was to take control of a situation that seemed out of control to the offender. In 31% (n = 17), the offender's motivation was to escape from the unbearable pain he was feeling. For 20% (n = 11), the offender's reason for committing suicide was because of his anger at himself, followed by his failures regarding work, marriage, children, financial (24%, n = 13), anger at others (15%, n = 8), problems in a relationship(s) (11%, n = 6), physical illness (9%, n = 5), and emotional/mental health problems (6%, n = 3).

x. *Five-Factor Model*

By analyzing statements in the notes, elements of the five-factor model were coded and designated at a high or low level. For 76% (n = 44) of the notes, at least one personality factor at a high level was coded, and for 38% (n = 22), at least one personality factor at a low level was coded. Table 3 displays the multiple responses according to the personality factor(s).

V. Discussion

a. Application of the Interpersonal–Psychological Theory to CSO Suicide

Not all CSOs choose to commit suicide. So how does a CSO get to the point of deciding to end his own life? Examining CSO suicide within the framework of the general suicide research is an important first step toward understanding why some CSOs choose suicide while others do not. One suicide model that has received an increasing amount of empirical support is the IPT (Joiner, 2005). The authors of this current study propose that CSOs in this sample were likely exhibiting all three features of Joiner's model, which include thwarted belongingness, perceived burdensomeness, and acquired capability at the time of the suicide.

i. Thwarted Belongingness

The authors observed that CSOs often feel different from others, knowing that their sexual interest in children is not acceptable to society. Once their crimes are exposed and their secret life is uncovered, they feel quite isolated, thus lacking a sense of belonging. The shame of the investigation might create a greater wedge between the family and the offender or might increase the offender's fear of anticipated loss of family. CSOs who are married and have children might feel an increased concern that the ensuing investigation would be a burden on their families.

Marriage and children typically provide a sense of belonging and are often reported as protective factors against suicide in the general population (Lester, 1999). Alternatively, individuals who are divorced, widowed, or single have an increased risk. However, it appears that being married or having children does not have the same protective impact on this population of CSOs. CSOs in this sample were as likely to be married as unmarried. In addition, since 60% of the sample had

T.A. Hoffer and J.L.E. Shelton, *Suicide Among Child Sex Offenders*,
SpringerBriefs in Psychology, DOI 10.1007/978-1-4614-5937-8_5,

© Springer Science+Business Media New York 2013

children and 59% lived with another person, they did not appear to be physically isolated from family members.

Interestingly, even though half the sample was married, the CSO's perception of belonging was not always on par with that factor. For example, some offenders wrote that they had pulled away from their family members (parents, siblings, and spouses) due to the sexual behaviors they were engaged in, such as the collecting of child pornography.

In addition, the condition of the marital relationship at the time of suicide may be more important than the marital status of the offender. This distinction is of particular interest, especially when a key component of lack of belonging is that previously meaningful relationships have become strained or lost (Joiner, 2005). For CSOs in this sample, experiencing recent marital or family conflict as a result of the pending investigation was quite common. In some cases, the spouses and children had already left the home and/or filed for separation or divorce. This undoubtedly created additional stress for the offender and even more uncertainty about his future.

Another possible contributor to a CSO's lack of belonging is the recent loss of his job or career due to the pending investigation. Over one-third of the CSOs in the current sample had been forced to resign, retire, asked to leave, or were fired from their job. Given that the CSOs in the sample were often middle-aged men with some form of higher education, they often had established jobs/careers that provided a sense of purpose and accomplishment. The loss of identity and status, as well as close relationships with colleagues, likely further contributed to his lack of belonging.

The following case example[1] highlights the aspect of lack of belonging and illustrates how the loss of family, job, and reputation influences some CSOs to choose suicide.

ii. Case Illustration 1

In 2008, Michael Stevenson went to a local store to have repairs done to computer. Stevenson was a highly educated, 38-year-old unmarried father of a recently adopted 12-year-old boy. As the store attendant examined the computer, he discovered pictures of nude and partially nude boys. The store attendant became concerned especially since Stevenson was a manager of a local youth serving organization. He returned the repaired computer to Stevenson a few days later but called local law enforcement and told them what he had discovered on Stevenson's computer. Local law enforcement then called federal authorities who executed a search warrant at his home several days later. Upon law enforcement's initial entry, Stevenson's 12-year-old son was found nude in his father's bed. Child Protective Services was called, and the child was removed from the home and taken into their custody.

[1] We have changed the names and other identifiers, such as location and specific details, in the case examples in order to protect the identity of the CSOs and their families.

Stevenson was interviewed during the course of the execution of the search warrant. He confessed that he had images of child pornography on his computer. A review of his computer revealed over 300 child pornography images and videos to include images he produced of his son. He also admitted ordering and receiving several videos which depicted images of corporal punishment of boys but denied ever using this type of discipline on his son. During the course of the search, officers discovered a locker in his garage and asked Stevenson for the combination. He provided the combination and advised that he kept the locker secure so that his son could not gain entry to it. He stated the locker contained sex items that were for his use with other adults and admitted that pain gave him sexual pleasure.

Upon opening the locker, law enforcement discovered a collection of various paddles, whips, chains, clamps, bondage gear, and straps. Law enforcement subsequently located video equipment and videos which depicted Stevenson engaged in corporal punishment of his son. In each of these video clips, his son was nude and Stevenson was spanking him with a wooden paddle and leather strip. When questioned, Stevenson denied this gave him sexual pleasure, but the videos clearly indicated that Stevenson had an erection.

At the completion of the search warrant, officers asked Stevenson about his emotional state and whether he would like to have a relative or close friend come to the residence. Stevenson denied suicidal ideation and advised he would call a close friend after they left. Shortly thereafter, Stevenson left his residence and drove a few hours away to a location where he rented a cabin. Sometime during his travels, he stopped at a store and purchased razors. Once in his cabin, he wrote a note which read, "Tommy (son), I am sorry & I love you so much. You are everything to me. Mom, Dad, and Sue (friend), – please forgive what I do. I love you as well and never wanted to bring shame to you or the (organization)."

Stevenson began cutting himself on his neck and arms. Cause of death was an incised wound to his left arm which severed the brachial artery. He was discovered dead the next morning by a maid.

As part of their investigation, law enforcement interviewed several coworkers and gathered background information and personality characteristics of Stevenson. His subordinates reported that Stevenson was a bully who had a hostile temper and ran off staff members with his behavior. Adjectives used by staff members to describe Stevenson were "abusive," "lunatic," and "control freak." He was also portrayed as self-conscious, but others also felt he thought he was the smartest person in the room. Stevenson was easily overwhelmed by stress and exhibited almost paranoid behavior regarding work decisions by reanalyzing every action he made.

Staff members also reported that Stevenson frequently commented on the physical characteristics of certain boys, describing them as "handsome" and would physically touch these boys by putting an arm around their shoulders, hugging, and holding hands. Some staff members described this behavior as "creepy" but felt they could not confront Stevenson about it due to his violent outbursts. Stevenson had also instructed his staff to bring all tough, troubled boys to his office for counsel. Stevenson would then talk with the boys in his office for long periods of time. He also appeared to be very proprietary of his relationship with his son, even becoming jealous of other adult males and females with whom his son interacted.

iii. Burdensomeness

Once aware of the investigation, CSOs often felt stigmatized and may have seen themselves as a burden to their families or even society and felt they had nothing to contribute. They may have also believed the disclosure of their offenses would humiliate and thus burden their family. Furthermore, many CSOs were concerned about losing their jobs and not being able to meet their financial obligations (e.g., mortgage, bills, health insurance, and child support). These possibilities not only would affect the offender's future but would also negatively impact his spouse and children, leaving him with an inability to contribute financially to the family and a sense of burdensomeness. He likely felt that he had now become a liability, and upon his death, some, if not all of these concerns, would disappear.

An additional factor that may have contributed to burdensomeness is the relatively common reporting of medical issues experienced by the CSO at the time of his death. In some cases, CSOs had a medical history that was long-standing and quite serious (e.g., multiple sclerosis, loss of limbs from diabetes, Parkinson's, cancer). For these individuals, there may have already been an established sense of burdensomeness prior to their awareness of the investigation. Interestingly, many CSOs in this sample, even those who had less serious medical conditions, discussed their medical issues in their suicide notes and often addressed them in the context of burdensomeness (e.g., "I have a medical condition and this way you won't have to take care of me").

iv. Acquired Capability

The third and final element of Joiner's IPT Model is acquired capability to completing suicide. An essential part to completing suicide is overcoming the physical pain (or fear of it) that is often associated with death. Acquired capability is developed over time due to repeated exposure to painful and provocative event. It remains relatively static and does not come and go over time (Joiner, 2005). Therefore, painful and provocative events from many years past as well as more recent painful experiences contribute to one's ability to commit suicide.

Past suicide research has highlighted the influential role health/medical problems can have on one's decision to commit suicide (Hendin, 1999); these were commonly reported among subjects in this sample. Chronic diseases, recent surgeries, and diagnoses of cancer, diabetes, and heart-related diseases were reported most often in the current sample. In addition to contributing to feelings of burdensomeness, an offender's medical issues may have increased his acquired capability to commit suicide due to the painful nature associated with many health-related problems. Additionally, chronic health problems can mentally prepare and thus, disinhibit one's fear of dying.

A rather unexpected finding by the authors was that military service, specifically veterans, were well represented in this sample, in nearly half of the known cases.

The following case example provides an illustration of cases where the CSO has past military service or is active military.

b. Case Illustration 2

In 2009, Samuel Hansen, an active member of the military, was interviewed by military investigators regarding his interest and criminal activities surrounding child pornography. He confessed that he had been accessing child pornography from the Internet for many years and reported that he had been sexually abused for many years by a male friend of his father's. The abuse continued for many years until Samuel reached adulthood and moved out of the house after joining the military.

The analysis of the computer images of child pornography uncovered numerous images depicting young boys similar to the age when the offender was abused. He denied that he had contact offenses with any male and/or female minors. Although Samuel's commanders were informed about the investigation, it was decided that Samuel would be allowed to return to his regular shift at work.

Over the course of several days both at work and when he was off duty, he wrote a suicide note reflecting his thoughts and feelings about the investigation and his life. He documented the days and times prior to his suicide. Although Samuel stated that the abuse he incurred influenced his later collecting of child pornography, he blamed himself for his actions and the impending suicide. He felt very disgusted with himself and ashamed of his behavior. He expected others to be disgusted with him as well. Besides being ashamed, he also stated that he felt weak and was too much of a coward to go on. He said he could not survive the investigation nor could he imagine being out of the military or having to return to the house where he was abused. He apologized to people and asked others to forgive him.

An interesting aspect of the note was that Samuel started to write his note days prior to his suicide. The specific days and times he noted were similar to journal entries. At times, he felt nauseated and dizzy. He made a number of suicide attempts which failed. One night, he put a bag over his head, but it ripped. Another time, he forgot to put the bag over his head when he went to sleep. He attempted to cut his wrists but realized that it was difficult to successfully die using this method. He presented practical information about what to do with his belongings and his body.

Samuel realized that in the midst of knowing that he would be taking his life, he began to appreciate life and spent time at the beach enjoying himself. As he got closer to his suicide, he discussed using a firearm is a sure way to die by suicide. He described the unsettled feeling of butterflies in his stomach, which he equated with getting pulled over by the police and getting a DUI. He experienced ambivalence about committing the suicide act, but he pessimistically stated that he would not have a future or anyone to love. Interestingly, Samuel waited to kill himself until he completed his scheduled detailed duty.

Recent research has proposed that military service may influence suicide behavior and increase acquired capability since combat and training exposes an individual to pain, fear, and death (Selby et al., 2010). Although war zone violence would be the greatest contributor to acquired capability, recent studies have shown that military training alone can increase one's ability to commit suicide (Bryan, Cukrowicz, West, & Morrow, 2010; Selby et al.). Military training exposes one to repeated injuries, use of violent weapons, simulated combat activities, and other intense situations which decreases one's fear of death and desensitizes one to pain (Joiner, 2005; Selby et al.). Familiarity and comfort level with firearms is also likely to be higher among military members. If one is trained in firearms, then using a gun to commit suicide may not invoke as much fear as other potential methods (Selby et al.). Compared to the current sample, in a separate FBI sample of CSOs who *did not* commit suicide, only 7% of the sample were current military or veterans (FBI, 2010). Although the offenders in both samples likely experienced lack of belonging and burdensomeness due to shame, anxiety, and fear, the CSOs who did not choose suicide may have lacked the acquired capability to commit suicide because of their deficits in painful and provocative experiences (e.g., military service). This distinction between two samples of CSOs may further support the importance of the acquired capability element among CSOs who choose suicide compared to those who do not.

Another possible contributor to acquired capability among this sample is the finding by the authors that some CSOs in this sample had previously contemplated suicide and had even made preparations for their suicide if or when law enforcement discovered their offenses. Prior research has found that mental rehearsals and/or daydreaming of death could increase one's acquired capability for suicide (Selby, Anestis, & Joiner, 2007). Some CSOs in this sample killed themselves just seconds after law enforcement knocked and announced their presence at their residences, indicating some degree of prior contemplation, planning, and even mental rehearsal. Furthermore, nearly one quarter of the sample committed suicide less than 48 hours after awareness of the investigation, suggesting that preparation for suicide may be more prevalent among certain CSOs.

In summary, the IPT of suicidal behavior makes two predictions: (1) that an individual's perceptions of burdening others and social alienation combine to instill the desire for death and (2) only those individuals who have experienced habituation to pain will develop the capability to kill themselves. This second prediction may be the most important in examining suicidality among CSOs because many, if not the overwhelming majority, of CSOs experience high levels of burdensomeness and lack of belonging once their sexual interest in children becomes known to others. Thus, through the lens of the IPT of suicide, one could surmise that nearly all CSOs at some point in their lives may have a desire to die and are potentially at risk for suicide. However, not all CSOs commit suicide. Many CSOs tolerate the loss of job, family, and home; navigate the legal proceedings; serve their sentence; and go on with their lives. For some, the investigation produces such anxiety, fear, and shame that their situation becomes intolerable and suicide becomes their preferred alternative. Thus, the CSOs who have experienced habituation to pain may be at the highest risk for suicide because they possess both elements of the IPT – desire and capability.

c. Analysis of Suicide Notes Left by CSOs

The analysis of the suicide notes included numerous aspects that have been found to be significant in other research examining suicide notes (Bhatia, Verma, & Murty, 2006; Darbonne, 1969; Foster, 2003; Ho, Yip, Chiu, & Halliday, 1998; Leenaars & Balance 1984; Lester, Wood, Williams, & Haines, 2004; Linn & Lester, 1996; McClelland, Reicher, & Both, 2000). The average estimated percentage of suicide notes among the general suicide population is approximately 25% (Joiner, 2010). Surprisingly, the percentage of CSOs that left a suicide note in the current sample is substantially higher (68%). When comparing the current sample of those who left suicide notes to those who did not (32%), researchers found no significant differences between the two groups. Variables compared were offender demographics, such as age, marital status, children, living status, education, employment, and incident offense category. Similarly, Foster found no significant differences in age, sex, marital status, current unemployment, prior history of self-harm, physical illness, contact with medical providers during the prior year, psychological disorders, use of psychotropic medication, method of suicide, life events, and living circumstances. Except for being more likely to live alone and less likely to live with nonfamily members, Callanan and Davis (2009) indicated that those who leave a note share many similarities with those who do not. For example, both groups were as likely to report depressions, bipolar disorder, or severe anxiety disorders to have been treated by a mental health provider or received medical treatment. Additionally, there were no differences between the two groups in the number of prior attempts or communicating suicidal intention; however, those who made a suicide threat were less likely to leave a suicide note. There were no differences in toxicology screenings between note writers and non-note writers, although note writers were more likely to have drugs at the scene.

In the BAU study, 85% of the CSOs addressed the note to a specific person or group (e.g., family and friends). This was significantly higher than the 35% obtained by Bhatia et al. (2006). Most frequently, the notes in the current sample were addressed to family members such as a spouse, girlfriend, children, and other family members. In some cases, notes were addressed to emergency personnel and law enforcement.

The authors theorize that for a CSO, leaving a note might be an important last chance to explain to his surviving family and friends why he was being investigated, to explain or deny his behavior, and to attempt to control the perceptions others might have about him. Additionally, CSOs who leave a suicide note might do so to alleviate some of the burden with which he believes his family will have to cope. This has been supported in the literature by Linn and Lester (1996) and Joiner et al. (2002).

As previously discussed, Joiner's (2005) IPT of suicide incorporates three factors: thwarted or lack of belonging, burdensomeness, and acquired capability. The suicide notes obtained from the current sample were initially reviewed for any evidence of the three variables in Joiner's model. The majority of the notes contained at least one element of the IPT (79%). Burdensomeness (54%) and lack of belonging (31%) were most frequently endorsed in the CSO sample. There were limited statements (15%) in the notes regarding whether the CSOs experienced prior situations that increased their acquired capability to take their lives. A few statements indicated CSOs had past experiences, which could have exposed and desensitized them to pain; these included references about going to the hospital, a recent health-related diagnosis, or experiences in the military through training and/or deployment. Other aspects present in the notes, which might also support Joiner's IPT model, were consideration of others, impression management, apology/forgiveness, shame, escape from intolerable pain (to die), anger at oneself (to be killed), and self-blame.

Individuals who commit suicide and leave a note often indicate blame toward themselves and/or others (Darbonne, 1969; Linn & Lester, 1996; McClelland et al., 2000). Self-blame was an aspect that was frequently endorsed in the current sample of suicide notes (78%). The aspect of self-blame might relate to the feelings of burdensomeness and low self-esteem. Individuals who accept blame for their actions might also be more likely to believe that their suicide will decrease the impact on others.

Blaming of others was also found to be a feature in over one-third of the notes (37%). The blaming of others is similar to "projection," which is defined as unpleasant impulses, stressors, ideas, or affects that are attributed to others and is often used to avoid responsibility (VandenBos, 2006).

The aspect of blame was also analyzed to see if individuals had a tendency to either place all of the blame on themselves or on others. The authors found that, in 71% of the cases where self-blame was present, blaming of others was not. And in 62% of the cases where the individuals blamed others, they did not also blame themselves. However, a small percentage (22%) blamed both themselves and others.

Cognitive distortions were analyzed in the suicide notes from the current sample and were found to be frequently expressed in this sample's suicide notes. Sixty-six percent of the sample endorsed at least one cognitive distortion. Cognitive distortions help CSOs separate from the actions they know are illegal and immoral in order to maintain a positive sense of self and to protect themselves from any anxiety and/or distress as a result of their criminal behavior. CSOs often minimize their sexual interest in children and rationalize that collecting and distributing child pornography does not harm children (Hoffer, Shelton, Behnke, & Erdberg, 2010; Lanning, 2010; Ward, 2000). Indicators of cognitive distortions were analyzed in the notes; these included denial, minimization, and rationalization. Some examples of denial included the statement "I have never harmed anyone and never would." An example of rationalization included "I'm not making any excuses as to why I am the way I am. When I was young I suffered a series of traumatic events."

Cognitive distortions may also explain why CSOs in this sample frequently left a suicide note behind. The suicide note was an opportunity for the CSOs to utilize impression management and attempt to influence how others might react to the investigation against them and their subsequent suicide. The most commonly endorsed cognitive distortion was minimization (42%). Following the search warrant or knock and talk interview, most likely CSOs cannot ignore the fact that they are under investigation. Minimization helps CSOs to decrease the impact of the allegations on the CSOs' loved ones.

Although denial was the least endorsed cognitive distortion (24%), in some way not addressing the investigation at all could be interpreted as a form of denial. Although 69% discussed the investigation in their notes, their statements were vague and indirect. Examples included “this is my fault that I got into this spot” or “we all make mistakes.” Very few offenders in the sample directly addressed the accusations against him or confessed to the crimes for which he was under investigation. The authors propose that this may be due to the fact that, in some cases, the suicide prevented the investigation from uncovering other crimes the offender may have committed. Through various interviews with investigators, the researchers developed a strong suspicion that the offender may have committed more child sex crime offenses than what was initially uncovered during the investigation (e.g., hands-on/contact offenses, additional victims).

Among the general population who leave suicide notes, Joiner et al. (2002) found that many included practical information, advice, or instructions. In the current sample, 74% provided practical information, including where others could find his body, a last will and testament, advice to others, and statements indicating how his loved ones should think about him after his death. For example, in one note, the CSO wrote, “Find me either down trail toward Douglas, or uptrail toward the creek edge…. Do not hook me up to any life-support please!!”

The overall tone of the suicide note was found in the sample to vary greatly. The majority of the offenders expressed love and affection for their loved ones; however, some notes in the sample had a detached tone. A note that was detached often lacked any emotional content and was typically shorter and more focused on practical matters, without any personal or intimate information.

The CSOs often offered an apology (69%) or request for forgiveness (41%) and expressed feelings of shame and/or guilt (59%). These statements referred to the investigation and the impending suicide. For example, “I love you and always will,” “How sorry I am for putting you all through this,” and “I'm ashamed and too much of a coward to go on.” During investigative interviews by law enforcement, many CSOs expressed feelings of guilt, self-loathing, and shame regarding their sexual arousal to children. Feelings of shame and a concern about getting caught influence CSOs to hide their actions from others, including those closest to them. This shame can cause CSOs to confess to their crimes during an interview; however, the CSOs also realize that their confessions will result in greater exposure regarding their criminal behaviors (Hoffer et al., 2010).

The emotion of anger toward others (to kill), a motive for suicide first offered by Karl Menninger (1938), was not frequently reported (15%) in the current sample of suicide notes. Examples of the few notes that indicated this anger toward others included statements like “they will not chain me and treat me like an animal,” “your father just wanted to tear this family apart and I could not take it!” and “I am hated by everyone for the way I was created. Just so you know, I hate you as well.”

Similar to the findings of Bhatia et al. (2006), the majority of the CSOs in the current sample indicated a reason for why they chose to die by suicide.

The most frequently cited reason was the CSO investigation (62%) and to take control (55%). In addition, 31% desired to escape from intolerable pain, and 20% were motivated by anger at themselves.

Interestingly, a number (21%) of the suicide notes contained specific details about the suicide act and the preparations for taking his life. For example, one CSO wrote, "this blade is a lot coarser than I thought. I am having a hard time cutting, self-preservation it seems to be working well," "a handgun is a sure and fast way to die," and "2 hours, God, not man, shall be my judge," "better to be free I begin to wonder if this will work." Additionally, some CSOs referenced life after death, and some thought differently about life as they prepared for death. For example, "P.S. If I come back to visit in the afterlife please welcome me and don't be afraid," "I never really took the time to really appreciate being alive…I wish I had more time."

The notes in the current sample indicated some additional interesting aspects. One of the CSOs referred to himself in the third person, contained within a fantasy he created in the note. A number of the notes indicated that the CSOs did not have the courage to go on and face the consequences. Some of the notes reminisced about past memories with the person to whom the note was addressed and expressed positive words that for the most part they had lived good lives. One individual included a number of poems to express his thoughts and feelings and one asked another relative to fix the spelling in his letter to his parents. Finally, one note used self-talk, "stop being a pussy. Man up" in order to build himself up or to mentally rehearse the act of suicide.

i. Examples of Aspects and Features Contained in the Suicide Notes

Self-Blame

"I'm very aware of how wrong I am."

"I apologize for all the anguish I may have caused to everyone. You have all become like family to me and for that I am sorry. Thanks for everything. Sorry for the anguish I have caused."

Blaming of Others

"Í have been a victim of circumstances coming together to create an intolerable situation."

"My wife wouldn't wear hot lingerie only wanted modest, private legal sex."

"My dad put the final nail in the coffin…but he was my only hope and he let me down once again, as he had all my life."

"I will not go to jail. I will not be labeled a 'sex offender' to have to register every move I make the rest of my life – to never have peace where I live or work."

Shame

"I'm ashamed and too much of a coward to go on."
"I'm gonna miss this place, if only my shame was concealed a little longer. I was starting to break away from it too."

"You're probably disgusted with who I turned out to be. I don't blame you."

"I can't live with who I am anymore."

Expressions of Love and Affection

"I love you more than anything in the world."

"You have been the light of my life. Leaving you has torn my soul apart. Always remember that I love you."

"As I sit here in my last few hours I keep thinking of how much I want to hold you in my arms and hug you."

Cognitive Distortions

Denial

"I never hurt anyone, but myself now."

"I know in my heart that I'm innocent. I did not do what they charged me with." "I'm not that kind of person, I never have been, never will be."

"I swear I have done nothing wrong."

Minimization

"In spite of all my mistakes, I love each of you deeply and forever."

"I am sorry for the way things have worked out."

"I had a problem and now the problem is taken care of."

Rationalization

"I'm not making any excuses as to why I am the way I am. When I was young I suffered a series of traumatic events."

"I never penetrated them. That's all they {victims} had to do is fight me and I would have stopped."

Joiner's (2005, 2010) Interpersonal-Psychological Theory (IPT)

Lack of Belonging "I can't imagine life out of the Military and to go back to Kansas, a house that never was a home is too painful." "I am an outcast to our society, to almost everyone."

Burdensomeness "It has nothing to do with you. Please don't blame yourself. I'm sorry about all the problems that am causing all of you." "I don't want to be a financial drain on you."

Acquired Capability "I think I have colon/rectal cancer and possibly prostate cancer, so this way of dying is probably better." "Twenty days of unrelenting pain. The only relief is merciful sleep."

Apology/Ask for Forgiveness

"I apologize for all the anguish I may have caused to everyone in medical. You have all become like family to me and for that I am sorry. Thanks for everything. Sorry for the anguish I have caused."

"How sorry I am for putting you all through this."

The Suicide Act

"I always wanted to learn how to bungee jump. I think the rope was suppose to be attached to the other end."

"Damn I failed, it seems the bag I taped over my head failed to kill me. It tore in my sleep and gave oxygen a chance to revitalize me. I thought it was the end, it certainly felt like it was. But how did the bag tear open?"

"I feel nauseated and seem to suffer from vertigo. This blade is a lot courser than I thought. I'm having a hard time cutting, self-preservation it seems… to be working."

Life After Death

"I know deep down that there is an afterlife. My greatest sadness in doing this is that I am banishing myself to an eternity without seeing your face ever again."

"There is one thing I am sure of, I won't be alone. It will be nice to see Grandma and Grandpa. God told me they were there 25 years ago."

"Please remember me on my date of death forever and I will always be happy with you."

The Investigation or Legal Process

"I've never had anything close to what dad had. Little boys being tied up, naked and raped by bigger men."

"Don't consider my death an admission of any charges and accusations against me."

Pessimism/Expecting a Bad Outcome

"They say life is just memories and anticipation. I have a lot of memories but nothing to look forward to."
"My job and profession are all I know and I'm too old to start over again. Too old and tired and hurt too much."

Subtle/Indirect Anger

Memo to County legal system: 'From hell's heart I stab at thee – For hate's sake I spit my last breath at thee' (direct quote from a poem).

d. Multidisciplinary Considerations

Initially, we aimed to assist law enforcement officers by increasing awareness of CSO suicide in the hope of mitigating the risk of suicide and enhancing operational strategies to include officer safety (Hoffer et al., 2010). The findings of this study may also inform prison/jail personnel as well as prosecutors and judges who make decisions regarding detention and seizure of weapons. In addition, given that on average, six people are impacted when a person commits suicide, mental health and community service providers that work with victims and family members/close associates of offenders may also benefit from an increased understanding of the broad spectrum of responses and reactions following a CSO's death by suicide.

i. Considerations for Law Enforcement

In this section, we will address the typical mindset of the law enforcement officer during interactions with CSOs and will offer considerations for law enforcement prior, during, and following the execution of a search, arrest warrant, or knock and talk with CSOs (Hoffer, Shelton, & Joyner, 2012).

CSOs are most likely processing a large amount of information during their initial contact with law enforcement and are experiencing tremendous stress, which impacts how they might respond during that contact. They are usually unprepared for this event and therefore will respond with some degree of stress. This stress response impacts the offenders' physiological, psychological, and behavioral reactions to the law enforcement officer. Unfortunately, law enforcement does not consistently apply the concepts of stress response during search and arrest warrants of CSOs due to the perception that CSOs are less dangerous and less violent.

In some cases, CSOs may consider acting out violently toward law enforcement or against themselves. They are likely considering a number of factors in their decision to act out: how many law enforcement officers respond to the scene; prior experience, skills, or abilities of law enforcement officers and the offender; access to weapons; mental state; their will to live and survive; and their ability to weigh the impact of each potential decision. The CSOs might be more focused on crimes they have committed of which law enforcement is unaware, as well as getting through the next few moments of the initial contact and how the search or arrest might impact their lives.

CSOs may pose an additional risk of danger to themselves due to the stigmatizing nature of the violation. It is not uncommon for offenders to state during interviews that they wished law enforcement were investigating them for any other crime, like drug trafficking or homicide. To some offenders, the loss of employment, home, reputation, and freedom, as well as family and friends, is intolerable, and suicide might be viewed as the preferred alternative. In the current study, almost half of the sample was married, and 60% had children. In addition, nearly half of the CSOs were college educated; 62% were employed. These factors indicate that the majority of the CSOs in the study had much to lose when the investigation revealed their sexual crimes involving children. When individuals are desperate, they become stressed and can frequently make decisions based on emotion, resulting in their actions becoming more unpredictable. This unpredictability stems from the extreme circumstances coupled with the offender's perceived potential to lose everything, which could result in the offender acting out in a violent manner.

An additional motivation for CSOs to become noncompliant or act out aggressively against law enforcement may be to prevent further disclosures of crimes that have yet to be revealed to law enforcement. There is a high rate of confession among child sex offenders during initial interviews with law enforcement (Seto, 2008). The perception by law enforcement is that this information is just the "tip of the iceberg," as the offender may only reveal what they think law enforcement already knows. This concept that CSOs continue to hide other criminal acts is supported by research results from a sample of 155 Internet-related child sex offenders who were incarcerated for online violations only, which revealed that 85% subsequently disclosed that they had also engaged in hands-on offenses with children after being administered a polygraph (Bourke & Hernandez, 2009).

Law enforcement may be less alert to the dangers of CSOs due to the mindset that they are unlikely to be violent and less dangerous. Therefore, the danger to law enforcement is often underestimated when initiating search/arrest warrants and "knock and talk" contacts with CSOs. The current study highlights the potential risk CSOs pose to themselves and also the potential danger to law enforcement officers. The possibility that CSOs will act out violently during interactions with law enforcement must always be considered.

The following case information highlights the stress response of CSOs and demonstrates the dangerousness these offenders can pose during their contact with law enforcement.

1. Case Illustration 3

Robert Snyder, age 50, lived in the Midwest with his wife and had recently started a new job as a driver for a local bus company. Several years earlier, he had been dishonorably discharged from the army after an AWOL (absence without leave) finding and served several months in a military jail. In addition, he had also been reprimanded for sexual harassment toward another soldier during his military service. According to his wife, Snyder had a very keen interest in pornography during most of their 25-year marriage. She denied ever discovering child pornography but stated it was commonplace for her to find adult pornography magazines around their home. She also indicated that their marriage was abusive at times and stated that Snyder had punched, kicked, and threatened to kill her in the past. In addition, throughout their marriage, there had been several accusations by children of inappropriate sexual behavior by Snyder. However, none of these accusations rose to the level where law enforcement was contacted. After one accusation, Mrs. Snyder threatened to leave him resulting in Mr. Snyder threatening to kill himself and placing an unloaded gun in his mouth.

In early 2005, a local police investigation revealed that Snyder was engaging in criminal activity related to child pornography. An undercover officer had received over 600 images of child pornography from Snyder over the course of several months. In addition, computer analysis conducted after the search warrant of his home revealed that Snyder had a child pornography collection of over 300,000 images and 4,000 videos. In May of 2005, local law enforcement executed a search warrant at his home. As the team identified themselves at the front door, Mr. Snyder's wife opened the door and the team observed Snyder running away from the door and running down a flight of stairs to the basement. The officers yelled out to Snyder telling him to come up the stairs. As officers carefully proceeded down the stairs, the team heard Snyder threatening to shoot himself. One officer soon was able to obtain a visual of Snyder and observed he was holding a firearm. Negotiations then began between Snyder and law enforcement for him to put his gun down. Another officer quickly went back upstairs and removed Mrs. Snyder and her 6-year-old nephew, whom she was babysitting, from the residence for their safety.

During the 15–20 minutes of negotiations, Snyder made several comments that indicated his state of mind was one of desperation, extreme agitation, and willingness to die. For example, he stated repeatedly that, "I've been through this before and I'm not going back to jail. I might as well just end it now." He also made several comments about this ending as a "suicide-by-cop." Soon after stating "I'm going to blow my brains out," Snyder, who was holding the gun against the side of his head, began moving the firearm away from his temple, and officers interpreted this action as his preparation to fire at the officers. In response to this hostile action, officers began firing at him. As Snyder was being shot by law enforcement, he simultaneously raised his weapon and shot himself in the mouth.

The following suggestions are focused on interactions law enforcement might have with CSOs, to include knock and talks, as well as execution of search and arrest warrants. Some of the more dangerous incidents reported have occurred when law enforcement attempted to make contact with the CSO after he did not show up for a court hearing. The suggestions listed below are considerations for law enforcement but are in no way legally mandated or required. The suggestions offered by the authors should be reviewed and approved by the law enforcement agency's management and/or legal counsel. These recommendations have been developed through the authors' investigative experiences with CSOs, along with discussions with numerous local, state, and federal law enforcement investigators across the country.

2. Prior to Contact with a CSO: Obtain Background Information

Prior to executing a search warrant or conducting a knock and talk at the CSO's residence, there are many steps law enforcement can take to better prepare the team (Hoffer et al., 2012). Efforts should be made to obtain any and all background information about the CSO, such as criminal history. Obtaining specifics about prior crime(s) can be helpful to law enforcement because it provides information on how the CSO might respond to law enforcement contact.

There is additional information law enforcement could obtain that might assist them in better evaluating how the CSO might respond to the initial contact. Based on the BAU's study, a large percentage of subjects who have committed suicide had prior military experience. Such individuals often maintain a strong sense of honor and an expectation of proper conduct. For the CSOs with a military background, these expectations might increase their feelings of shame and guilt. Military history could also elevate the possibility that the CSO has firearms in his residence or has experience with the use of firearms.

Additionally, law enforcement should look for any information that indicates that the CSO is isolated, feels alone, or tends to be a loner, based on his living situation, type of employment, or lack of activity or contact with others. Conducting a surveillance might reveal if he has contact with others, which could be a source of support to help him through the investigative process or might make the CSO think he will be a burden on them. Information indicating that the CSO may react to the investigation as if he is a burden on others, such as his family, would be helpful for law enforcement to understand. High conscientiousness, being an upstanding citizen who is well respected in the community, duty and honor bound, and a lack of criminal history could indicate that the CSO might feel he has a lot to lose and does not want to burden his family or besmirch his reputation.

Information about gun ownership or hunting licenses by conducting surveillance to determine activities in which the CSO is involved that include the use of firearms could be obtained by law enforcement. Law enforcement frequently makes a ruse phone call to obtain information about the CSO's Internet service provider. In addition, law enforcement could also obtain information about what activities or organizations in which the CSO is involved which might increase his acquired capability to take his life.

3. Prior to Contact with a CSO: Operational Plan and Briefing

The execution of most search warrants includes an operational plan that covers the pertinent information about the CSO and his residence, as well as any contingencies law enforcement might make (Hoffer et al., 2012). Employ a best practices approach, incorporating the most effective tactical steps to keep the team safe, such as wearing a vest at all times during contact with the CSO. The authors have interviewed a number of agents and officers in the field who report that safety vests were not always used during the execution of search warrants and even less frequently utilized during knock and talks. For officer safety, it is clearly advocated that vests, even undercover vests, be utilized during every interaction with CSOs.

In the FBI BAU sample of 106 offenders, 10% of the cases posed a danger to the law enforcement officers affecting the search or arrest warrant. Some teams might need additional training regarding how to respond when the search team knocks and announces themselves at the CSO's door and they hear a gun shot. Consideration could be given to notifying the SWAT and Crisis Negotiation Team about the upcoming operation being executed at the offender's location; this prepares them in the event the CSO responds aggressively toward law enforcement or toward himself.

Simply by completing an operational plan, officers are better prepared to successfully resolve a dangerous situation. If time does not permit a written arrest plan to be completed, at a minimum, a verbal arrest plan should be briefed to all participants depending upon the law enforcement agency's protocol. A briefing entails a thorough explanation of the entire arrest plan to the arrest team and supporting personnel and can include how to identify and address any potential risk factors for suicide or other violent acts during the execution of the warrant. Clarity and confidence in a plan comes from knowing the roles of everyone involved. An additional benefit is that any deficiencies in the plan can be identified and addressed prior to approach or entry. To ensure all officers clearly understand their roles and responsibilities, a proper briefing and brief-back is typically conducted. Law enforcement should carefully weigh how the different approaches and tactical responses will impact the offender's cooperation during the investigation, agreement to submit to the interview, and/or consent to search and take the computer. It is important to weigh these issues along with officer safety.

A thorough briefing should include a discussion of the unique risk factors related to CSOs, including the potential for suicide. For example, the shame and embarrassment of being found out might increase a CSO's feelings of desperation and the perception that he will lose everything, such as his job, wife, children, friends, financial security, and self-image. He most likely has struggled with prior feelings of stress, anxiety, and internal conflict from his sexual arousal to children, downloading child pornography, and/or molesting children, which could have contributed to prior suicidal ideations, gestures, or attempts. He may have already thought about getting caught and might have made mental or actual preparations for his response to law enforcement. He might react with desperation, which could increase his instability and potential risk to himself and others. Law enforcement should be briefed about the risk that suicidal people could pose to others around them, including law enforcement. Any specific background information that was uncovered during the planning stages which might increase the CSO's risk for acting out violently against him or others should be emphasized. One member of the team could be identified who would be responsible for talking with the CSO to de-escalate the situation or to explore potential suicide or violence risk factors.

4. Initial Contact and De-escalation

Upon executing search/arrest warrants or at the initiation of a knock and talk, law enforcement officers should be mindful of not letting their guard down and should continually be looking for any signs indicating the potential for violence by the CSO against others or himself (Hoffer et al., 2012). Officers should quickly assess the best way to de-escalate the CSO's fight or flight response by eliciting more rational or objective thinking.

Unfortunately, when law enforcement officers perceive CSOs as posing little to no danger, they treat these situations with much less caution. This mindset leaves law enforcement unprepared if the CSO attempts to flee, resist arrest, or use deadly force and can reduce one's ability to prepare for an effective tactical response. Examples of complacency include not wearing a protective vest during the execution of a search warrant or knock and talk, allowing the CSO to walk around his residence during the execution of a search warrant, not checking the CSO's residence thoroughly for any potential danger, such as firearms, and allowing the CSO to do certain things such as going to the restroom or putting his dog away. Having the mindset that this offender, or any offender, could injure or kill the officer or someone else could reduce the risk to law enforcement.

Initially, the offender should be handcuffed for officer safety and placed in a secure area until any and all weapons can be secured. The offender should not be allowed to freely roam around the area. Ask the offender if there are any firearms in his residence and secure the firearm, perhaps by placing it in a law enforcement officer's vehicle until the team clears the residence. From anecdotal reports, it appears the risk for suicide of the CSO or a suicide-by-cop scenario might be greater than the risk to law enforcement.

The initial contact with the CSO allows law enforcement a preliminary observation of the offender's demeanor and reaction. As with other law enforcement contacts, the goal is to slow down the process and decrease the heightened emotions which might be elicited. Increase the CSO's ability to make rational decisions by engaging in ways that decrease his stress response, such as getting him to cooperate and agree to be interviewed by law enforcement. If the offender refuses to be interviewed and wants to leave the residence during the search, consider posting an agent or officer at the front of the residence in case the offender returns.

5. Interview of the CSO

For most situations in which law enforcement is contacting a CSO, an interview is vital to obtain additional information and evidence of the CSO's criminal activity. The interview can also offer law enforcement an opportunity to obtain information about additional stressors and potential risk factors for violence (Hoffer et al., 2012). In addition, the interview may provide potential themes for building rapport with the CSO and/or use if the contact results in a barricade situation and negotiations become necessary.

Consider separating the interview of the CSO into two parts. The initial focus would be on conducting the interview and interrogation regarding the CSO's criminal activities; the second would focus on asking pertinent questions regarding the CSO's state of mind, his support system, and any risk factors related to suicide. If the same law enforcement officer is not able to conduct both phases, consider identifying a law enforcement officer who is able to conduct this specialized interview.

Law enforcement should discuss with the CSO how he will be specifically impacted by this investigation and carefully observe his reactions or even lack of responses to these questions. Some investigators interviewed in the BAU's study discussed how the offenders who later died by suicide were extremely shut down, did not talk much, and almost seemed "resigned."

It is not uncommon for people to think that asking someone about suicide could prompt the person to choose suicide. Research has shown this is not true (Bongar, 2002; Gould et al., 2005; Joiner, 2005). One of the strongest predictors of suicide attempts is "resolved plans and preparations" (Joiner, p. 207). During the interview with the CSO, ask him directly if he has ever thought about suicide or has attempted suicide. Obtain information regarding any past suicidal behavior, such as when he attempted suicide, what triggered the incident, and the details of his suicide attempt. Ask the CSO what occurred that resulted in him surviving the attempt. Ask the CSO directly if he is thinking about suicide now. Consider asking the offender if he is currently in therapy and obtain consent to contact his therapist and/or a family member to obtain support for the CSO and notify them about the potential risk for suicide.

6. Restricting Access to Firearms

There is evidence that restricting access to lethal weapons is an effective way to prevent suicide. The data come from studies that have uncovered statistically significant associations between death by suicide and household firearm ownership (Miller, Lippmann, Azrael, & Hememway, 2007). Case-controlled studies have found that persons who died by suicide were more likely to live in homes with firearms than in matched living and dead control groups (Kellerman, et al., 1992; Kung, Pearson, & Wei, 2005).

If approved and authorized, law enforcement should seize any firearm(s) located in the CSO's residence (Hoffer et al., 2012). If the firearm cannot be seized, law enforcement should consider other alternatives for restricting the CSO's access to firearms. A variety of options were discussed by investigators who were interviewed for this project and included removing the magazine and bullets from the firearm, giving weapons to family members or the CSO's attorney, taking them into evidence, and holding the firearm until proper ownership could be confirmed. If the search was based on a federal warrant, consider requesting the local law enforcement task force member to maintain the firearm until it can be given to a responsible family member or the offender's attorney. Law enforcement should consult with their legal counsel before employing these options.

Although restricting firearms among certain individuals or in certain areas of the country (e.g., those specifically training to use them and for whom the use of firearms may be a function of their job) may seem daunting or impossible, another option is to simply express your concerns to him about his state of mind and ask/persuade the CSO to give consent to remove the firearm. One recent study by the Veterans Health Administration, for example, found that suicidal persons during a time of crisis found it acceptable for clinicians to ask about firearm ownership, distribute trigger locks, and even provide safe offsite storage of firearms (Roeder et al., 2009). Finally, law enforcement should be aware that there may be a legal justification to removing the firearm if, for example, certain misdemeanor offenses are on the CSO's criminal record. The 1996 Lautenberg amendment (Pub. L. 104-208 S658) to the Gun Control Act of 1968 (Pub. L. 90-168) restricts those convicted of an act of misdemeanor domestic violence offense from shipping, transporting, possessing, or receiving firearms and ammunition. This rule applies to civilian and military personnel and to firearms and ammunition used for either personal or professional purposes (Ramchand, Acosta, Burns, Jaycox, & Pernin, 2011).

Moreover, the data and findings in this study could be utilized by law enforcement to support arguments for restricting the CSO's access to the firearm (keeping in mind that nearly 50% of the CSOs in this sample used firearms to take their lives). Other studies may also assist in providing justification for restricting the CSO's access to firearms. For example, Pritchard and King (2005) found that subjects who sexually offended against children were 183 times more likely to commit suicide compared to the general population. Seizing firearms is not only for the offender's safety but also for the safety of the team both during the initial contact with law enforcement and any subsequent contact (e.g., returning for arrest warrant and/or compliant/noncooperation with legal mandates). Finally, prior to leaving the residence, obtain the layout of the residence in order to address future contingencies if and when the team returns to affect an arrest warrant or address other legal issues.

7. After Contact with a CSO

After completing the search, the CSO is left with the full weight of the future legal process and the exposure of his sexual activities. He has time to think about other alternatives to being incarcerated. Depart from the residence expeditiously in order to prevent any potential altercation with the offender. Some agents and officers that were interviewed for the project indicated that at times, law enforcement teams stood outside discussing the case instead of leaving immediately (Hoffer et al., 2012). Consider contacting local law enforcement after leaving the CSO's residence, and advise them of any concerns regarding potential risk for violence. As a result, in the event they receive an emergency call from the residence, responding officers can be more prepared for what they may encounter.

If the CSO's firearm was seized by law enforcement, secure the weapon in evidence or other safe location and document the reason for the seizure, such as offender safety, to check on the serial number of the firearm or if the firearm was not legally owned by the offender. The prosecuting attorney can argue at the court hearing to maintain the weapon due to the CSO's potential risk of violence or suicide as well as to detain the CSO for his own safety and the safety of others close to him. The study conducted by the FBI's BAU can be utilized to support the argument to remove the firearm(s) from the CSO's residence. Consider contacting the CSO's therapist or family member about any concerns you have regarding the CSO's state of mind or potential for violence.

As previously mentioned, consider and plan for factors that could impact law enforcement if and when the team returns to the residence to affect the arrest of the offender. For example, note the layout of the residence and any potential tactically dangerous areas. In addition, be aware of factors related to the CSO that might increase officer safety when returning to arrest the CSO, such as comments in which he indicated that he has much to lose or that his wife would leave him if he went to jail. It is important to note that Brophy (2003) found in his study that each step along the legal path creates a period of increased risk for the sex offender and poses a potential challenge for law enforcement. Therefore, law enforcement should consider the offender's risk for suicide during subsequent contacts with the offender, as well.

ii. Considerations for the Legal Process

The number of defendants charged with child exploitation offenses, such as child pornography, sex transportation, and sex abuse, is a fast-growing segment of the federal criminal caseload in the USA (Byrne, Lurigio, & Pimentel, 2009; Motivans, 2007). Along with the increased number of defendants charged with sex crimes, the types of sex crimes that are federally prosecuted have also expanded (Byrne et al., 2009; Motivans). For example, in 1994, sex abuse or contact sexual offenses comprised 74% of all sex exploitation cases (Motivans). By 2006, sexual contact offenses constituted only 16% (Motivans). During that same period, child pornography cases increased from 22% in 1994 to 69% in 2006 (Motivans).

Due to increasing caseloads and the potential risk for suicide among child sex crime defendants, suicide prevention is likely to become a growing responsibility of court systems around the USA. This new responsibility will require the courts to reexamine their definitions of risk. In addition, the court system should include the potential for suicide when determining risk classifications, since the findings in the current study, as well as other studies, indicate that CSOs should be regarded by personnel of the judicial system both inside and outside the prison as having heightened risk for suicide (Brophy, 2003; Hoffer et al., 2010).

As a rule, the federal court system relies more heavily on pretrial detention than do state counterparts (Byrne & Stowell, 2007). Defendants charged federally with sexual exploitation offenses are typically released at the pretrial stage at a higher rate than federal defendants of other crimes (Byrne et al., 2009). In 2006, 53% of sex crime defendants were released prior to trial because they were assessed and classified to be at low risk for absconding or committing a new offense while on pretrial release (Byrne et al.). This assessment is generally correct – a very small percentage of sex crime defendants commit new violations while under supervision (Byrne et al.; Motivans, 2007). While these defendants are a low risk for committing new offenses prior to trial, pretrial release may actually increase their risk for suicide. Sex crime defendants may be less likely to be assessed for suicide and receive services to lower the risk for suicide. Also, they have more potential access to firearms and other weapons and cannot be watched as consistently as defendants who are detained. Prosecutors should consider adding the concern for the CSO's safety as an additional argument to detain the CSO for his own protection. In addition, it is suggested that when judges are weighing flight risk and future criminal activity for pretrial release, they also expand beyond the traditional risk criteria and consider the defendant's potential for self-harm.

Unfortunately, no nationwide estimates of suicide attempts or completions among federal pretrial sex crime defendants exist. This problem gained attention in two California federal districts after numerous suicides occurred among defendants charged with possession of child pornography. Under the traditional definitions of risk, these defendants were classified as low risk, as the majority of the defendants had no criminal or mental health history. The defendants' high risk of self-injury was ignored under the established risk classification system. In response, the US Pretrial Services Office in the Central District of California established a pilot program to lower the risk of suicide among sex crime defendants. The program allows for a multidisciplinary approach, with mental health providers and the criminal justice system working together in crisis intervention, therapy, and incarceration preparations (Byrne et al., 2009).

At the initial court appearance, the defendant is immediately referred for a psychological assessment and evaluated for depression, anxiety, and suicidal ideation. If the defendant meets the criteria for inclusion, he participates in weekly group sessions with other pretrial sex offense defendants. These individuals benefit from the support of others who are experiencing similar feelings and learn to manage the stress of the federal judicial process. Cognitive behavioral therapy is also utilized in order to reduce or eliminate catastrophic thinking patterns (e.g., "I will never find job when released from prison"; "I will get killed in prison"). In addition, defendants are prepared for the prison system through education of facilities, procedures, and policies. Even given some limitations, the program has seen success. Over 100 defendants have been referred to the program, and to date, all have self-surrendered to federal authorities, and none have committed suicide.

As the findings of the BAU study reflect, a heightened period of suicide risk for CSOs is shortly after becoming aware of the investigation. Of the 106 CSOs examined in this study, 55% killed themselves during the investigation period, defined as the time between awareness and before arrest. The program established by US Pretrial Services Office only identifies defendants upon their initial court appearance. As a result, a population of CSOs who may be at risk for suicide is being overlooked for any intervention or support. Since 43% of the CSOs examined in the current study committed suicide during the judicial process, theoretically, a program similar to the one described may have lowered their risk for suicide.

The military's suicide prevention efforts may offer some instruction to the criminal justice system on how to reduce the risk for suicide among those who kill themselves prior to arrest. The Air Force Suicide Prevention Program (AFSPP) established policies and procedures after determining that the time following an airman's arrest or investigative interview is a high-risk period for suicide (Ramchand et al., 2011). Investigators are required after any investigative interview to notify the airman's commander or supervisor in person. Those appearing emotionally distraught after an interview are released only to their commander or supervisor (Ramchand et al.). It then becomes the unit representative's decision to assess the individual's emotional state and contact a behavioral health provider if there is an indication of suicidal thoughts. Agencies without legal rights to detain an individual must make reasonable efforts to "hand off" the individual to a member of his or her unit or make notification as soon as possible if a handoff is not feasible. If the unit leader determines that the individual is at risk for suicide, he or she is required to accompany the individual to a helping agency for professional care.

Developing suicide prevention programs and/or policies for those being investigated for child sex crimes is challenging because it requires targeting individuals who may have never before displayed suicidal behavior but are thought to be at elevated risk for death by suicide. Further research is needed to determine which CSOs are a higher risk for suicide and who would benefit from suicide prevention programs/policies.

iii. Considerations for Mental Health and Community Service Providers

Sexual abuse, when disclosed, can cause significant psychological stress for all involved, especially for victims. Child sexual abuse victims often experience psychological and/or physical trauma that can have a lasting and pervasive impact over their lifetime (Terr, 2003). Victims exhibit a range of symptoms and negative emotions with varying intensity to include ambivalence and conflict regarding the sexual abuse (Terr). Depending on the type of relationship they had with the CSO, victims might be angry and scared of the offender but may also feel equally attached to him. A study of girls who were sexually abused by adult males found that half of the victims felt closely bonded or in love with the offender (Wolak, Finkelhor, & Mitchell, 2004). Lanning (2010) described this type of victim as a compliant victim, because he/she often receives time, attention, affections, gifts, money, and perception of love from the offender resulting in the victim being co-opted into the sexual contact. As a result, a more positive relationship develops but one that will likely complicate the victim's reactions to the offender's suicide.

Victims likely experience tremendous internal conflicts following an offender's suicide, although there is a lack of empirical research regarding victims' reactions. Walford, Kennedy, Manwell, and McCune (1990) found that incest victims often have to process the impact of the abuse as well as how the offender's suicide affects their lives. Other possible reactions may include taking the blame for causing the offender's suicide, relief that the offender is dead, and feeling guilt for such relief. On the other hand, victims could be angry that they did not receive justice from the anticipated court proceedings. Victims might relive the abuse, thus increasing their risk for suicide (Briere & Runtz, 1986). Finally, victims may experience loss due to the CSO's death, especially if they felt attached to the offender. Victims might feel pressure from others not to express this sense of loss or any positive feelings about the CSO.

In addition, the CSO's suicide can have a profound effect on the offender's family members (Hoffer et al., 2010). It is not uncommon for relatives and close friends to feel anger, sadness, and shock, particularly when the death is a result of a suicide. For these survivors, their loved one's suicide has a tremendous impact on them and the loss is often painful. Previous research indicated that the long-term effects of suicide on the bereaved are more problematic as compared to other forms of deaths (Ness & Pfeffer, 1986; Worden, 1996). The impact of the suicide is compounded when the deceased has committed sexual crimes against children. In some situations, the family, friends, or coworkers may have suspected or known about the offender's sexual interest in children. As a result, these individuals may experience some sense of responsibility or guilt. In other cases, family and friends may be completely unaware or in denial of the offender's sexual interest in children. In these instances, not only have they lost the actual presence of their relative or friend, but they might also experience cognitive dissonance whereby the inconsistent information creates an internal struggle within them. They may be left wondering if they ever really knew who their loved one was or if their entire relationship was built on lies.

Following the initial shock of the disclosure regarding the offender's activities and his suicide, it is not uncommon for some loved ones to minimize the offender's negative qualities or even deny the evidence that the offender committed crimes against children. As observed in some cases, family members believed that the offender committed suicide due to the stress of having his reputation ruined from a false allegation of child sex crimes. Family members are left to reconcile the crimes that the offender committed with the feelings of loss experienced when he dies. Such attempts to reconcile conflicting emotions can be expressed in the form of anger at the offender for committing these crimes and for destroying their life as they knew it, at the offender for killing himself and leaving them to deal with the media scrutiny, or at law enforcement for investigating their family member.

VI. Conclusion

This study is the beginning of an important discussion about the unique and complex issues surrounding CSOs who commit suicide. By overlaying already established suicide theories with the complexities of child sex offending, the authors hope to highlight why some CSOs choose to commit suicide. With cognitive distortions no longer protecting them, some offenders cannot tolerate the pending catastrophic loss of job, family, and reputation and see suicide as their only solution. Similarly, the CSOs' suicide notes reflect individuals who felt trapped and found suicide to be the only way to regain control and escape the intolerable pain of being exposed to the world as a CSO.

While we were not able to assess the prevalence rate of CSO suicide, this chapter does help substantiate anecdotal reports of an increased risk for suicide among this population of offenders. In addition, even though analysis on this topic has been limited, possibly due to society's conflicting reactions about the suicides of those who live in ways counter to cultural and social norms, this chapter is a considerable first step toward establishing a more effective crisis response and mitigating the risk for suicide among CSOs (Hoffer, Shelton, Behnke, & Erdberg, 2010). Finally, by providing empirical data and multidisciplinary considerations, the authors hope to increase awareness of CSO suicide among the various entities which come into contact with this population of offenders.

T.A. Hoffer and J.L.E. Shelton, *Suicide Among Child Sex Offenders*,
SpringerBriefs in Psychology, DOI 10.1007/978-1-4614-5937-8_6,
© Springer Science+Business Media New York 2013

VII. Future Research Directions

It is hoped that in the future an accurate prevalence rate of suicide among CSOs can be obtained in order to evaluate the likelihood a CSO will commit suicide. A comparison of the suicide CSO sample and a sample of offenders who chose not to commit suicide could assist investigators, attorneys, mental health professionals, correctional officers, and probation/parole in identifying risk factors for suicide among this unique population. In addition, the authors hope that this study will prompt additional research in other pertinent areas to include the following: (1) examining the degree that personality disorder symptoms increase risk for suicide among CSOs, (2) how the presence of cognitive distortions impact a CSO's decision to commit suicide, and (3) further examination of suicide notes written by CSOs.

The future for the FBI's BAU study will include completing interviews with the CSO's family members and/or close associates for the remaining cases. In addition, further analyses will be conducted to obtain potential typological information indicating more salient risk factors for this population. The authors will also be drafting volume two of a law enforcement handbook that will focus on conducting a risk interview with the CSO during the initial investigation.

T.A. Hoffer and J.L.E. Shelton, *Suicide Among Child Sex Offenders*,
SpringerBriefs in Psychology, DOI 10.1007/978-1-4614-5937-8_7,
© Springer Science+Business Media New York 2013

VIII. Limitations of the Study

Due to the selection of cases from the FBI's Automated Case Support, the sample was not randomly selected. The method of identifying subjects included specific query terms to isolate potential suicides. Following the offender's suicide, law enforcement investigators would most likely fill out the appropriate documentation to close the file. If the offender's suicide was not specifically documented using one of the search terms, the case might not have been identified. Additionally, due to the size constriction, this sample does not accurately represent suicides across the country, and hence, the suicides of CSOs cannot be generalized to other similar offenders.

The authors were not able to obtain an accurate prevalence rate for this population due to the lack of information regarding the number of law enforcement contacts with CSOs from knock and talks and execution of search or arrest warrants. To date, this information has not been obtained from the FBI database.

In addition, the sample is unique based on the fact that the majority of the sample was obtained from the FBI's database and may not be representative of all CSOs being investigated by local, state, and other federal law enforcement agencies. Finally, the use of the GAQ for this study relies on information obtained from third parties, whose insights and reflections of the CSOs are likely to contain a degree of positive or negative bias.

T.A. Hoffer and J.L.E. Shelton, *Suicide Among Child Sex Offenders*,
SpringerBriefs in Psychology, DOI 10.1007/978-1-4614-5937-8_8,

© Springer Science+Business Media New York 2013

IX. The FBI's Behavioral Analysis Unit III: Crimes Against Children

BAU III, a component of the FBI's Critical Incident Response Group (CIRG) National Center for the Analysis of Violent Crime (NCAVC), provides specialized behaviorally based operational support to federal, state, local and international law enforcement agencies involved in crimes against children. BAU III is comprised of Supervisory Special Agents and Professional Staff who are leading authorities in behavioral crimes involving child victims. Through the process of Criminal Investigative Analysis, BAU III reviews and assesses the facts of a criminal act and interprets offender behavior and victim/offender dynamics during the commission of the crime or as displayed at the crime scene.

BAU III services are provided at no cost to the requesting agency and are primarily coordinated through a network of NCAVC Coordinators located in FBI field offices throughout the country. Law enforcement and prosecutors can request BAU III services directly or by contacting the NCAVC Coordinator in their local FBI field office.

T.A. Hoffer and J.L.E. Shelton, *Suicide Among Child Sex Offenders*,
SpringerBriefs in Psychology, DOI 10.1007/978-1-4614-5937-8_9,
© Springer Science+Business Media New York 2013

References

Abel, G. G., Gore, D. K., Holland, C. L., Camps, N., Becker, J. V., & Rathner, J. (1989). The measurement of the cognitive distortions of child molesters. *Sexual Abuse: A Journal of Research and Treatment, 2*, 135–152.

Abel, G. G., Mittleman, M. S., & Becker, J. V. (1985). Sex offenders: Results of assessment and recommendations for treatment. In M. H. Ben-Aron, S. J. Hucker, & C. D. Webster (Eds.), *Clinical criminology: The assessment and treatment of criminal behavior* (pp. 207–220). Toronto, Canada: M & M Graphics.

Ahlers, C. J., Schaefer, G. A., Mundt, I. A., Rolle, S., Englert, H., Willich, S. N., & Beier, K. M. (2009). How unusual are the contents of paraphilias? Paraphilia-associated sexual arousal patterns in a community-based sample of men. *The Journal of Sexual Medicine, 8*, 1362–1370.

American Association of Suicidology. (2003). Knowing the warning signs. Retrieved July 8, 2010, from http://www.suicidology.org/web/guest/stats-and-tools/warning-signs

American Psychiatric Association. (2000). *Diagnostic and statistical manual of mental disorders: DSM-IV-TR*. Washington, DC: Author.

American Psychiatric Association. (2012). DSM-5: The future of psychiatric diagnosis, paraphilias, U 03 Pedophilic Disorder. Retrieved January 21, 2012, from http://www.dsm5.org/ProposedRevision/Pages/proposedrevision.aspx?rid=186

Ashton, M. C., Lee, K., & Goldberg, L. R. (2004). A hierarchical analysis of 1,710 personality descriptive adjectives. *Journal of Personality and Social Psychology, 87*, 707–721.

Baechler, J. (1979). *Suicides*. New York, NY: Basic Books.

Baumeister, R. F., & Leary, M. R. (1995). The need to belong: Desire for interpersonal attachments as a fundamental human motivation. *Psychological Bulletin, 117*, 497–529.

Beautrais, A. L., Joyce, P. R., & Mulder, R. T. (1999). Personality traits and cognitive styles as risk factors for serious suicide attempts among young people. *Suicide & Life-Threatening Behavior, 29*, 37–47.

Bhatia, M. S., Verma, S. K., & Murty, O. P. (2006). Suicide notes: Psychological and clinical profile. *International Journal of Psychiatry in Medicine, 36*, 163–170.

Black, S. T., & Lester, D. (1995). Distinguishing suicide notes from completed and attempted suicides. *Perceptual and Motor Skills, 81*, 802.

Blatt, J. (1995). Kohut's self-object for understanding psychological development, or 'what have you done for me lately?'. *PsycCRITIQUES, 40*, 840–843.

Bongar, B. M. (2002). *The suicidal patient: Clinical and legal standard of care*. Washington, DC: American Psychological Association.

Bostwick, J. M., & Pankratz, V. S. (2000). Affective disorders and suicide risk: A reexamination. *The American Journal of Psychiatry, 157*, 1925–1932.

T.A. Hoffer and J.L.E. Shelton, *Suicide Among Child Sex Offenders*,
SpringerBriefs in Psychology, DOI 10.1007/978-1-4614-5937-8,
© Springer Science+Business Media New York 2013

Bourke, M., & Hernandez, A. (2009). The 'Butner Study' redux: A report of the incidence of hands-on child victimization by child pornography offenders. *Journal of Family Violence, 24*, 183–191.

Briere, J., & Runtz, M. (1986). Suicidal thoughts and behaviors in former sexual abuse victims. *Canadian Journal of Behavioural Science, 18*, 413–423.

Brophy, J. (2003). Suicide outside of prison settings among males under investigation for sex offenses in Ireland during 1990 to 1999. *The Journal of Crisis Intervention and Suicide Prevention, 24*, 155–159.

Bryan, C., Cukrowicz, K., West, C., & Morrow, C. (2010). Combat experiences and the acquired capability for suicide. *Journal of Clinical Psychology, 66*, 1044–1056.

Buck, R. (1999). The biological affects: A typology. *Psychological Review, 6*, 301–336.

Butcher, J. N., & Megargee, E. I. (2001). *Minnesota multiphasic personality inventory-2*. San Antonio, TX: Pearson Education.

Byrne, J., Lurigio, A., & Pimentel, R. (2009). New defendants, new responsibilities: Preventing suicide among alleged sex offenders in federal pretrial system. *Federal Probation, 73*, 40–44.

Byrne, J. M., & Stowell, J. (2007). Examining the link between institutional and community violence: Toward a new cultural paradigm. *Aggression and Violent Behavior, 12*, 552–563.

Callanan, V. J., & Davis, M. S. (2009). A comparison of suicide note writers with suicides who did not leave notes. *Suicide & Life-Threatening Behavior, 39*, 558–568.

Card, J. J. (1974). Lethality of suicidal methods and suicide risk: Two distinct concepts. *Omega: Journal of Death & Dying, 5*, 37–45.

Cattell, R. B., Cattell, K., & Cattell, H. E. P. (2000). *16 PF* (5th ed.). San Antonio, TX: Pearson Education.

Cavanagh, J. T. O., Carson, A. J., Sharpe, M., & Lawrie, S. M. (2003). Psychological autopsy studies of suicide: A systematic review. *Psychological Medicine, 33*, 395–405.

Chance, S., Kaslow, N., & Baldwin, K. (1994). Anxiety and other predictors of severity of suicidal intent in urban psychiatric inpatients. *Hospital & Community Psychiatry, 45*, 716–718.

Chynoweth, R. (1977). The significance of suicide notes. *The Australian and New Zealand Journal of Psychiatry, 11*, 197–200.

Cohen, L., Nikiforov, K., Gans, S., Poznansky, O., McGeoch, P., Weaver, C., King, E. G., Cullen, K., & Galynker, I. (2002). Heterosexual male perpetrators of childhood sexual abuse: A preliminary neuropsychiatric model. *The Psychiatric Quarterly, 73*, 313–336.

Cole, M. (1990). Cultural psychology: A once and future discipline? In J. J. Bergman (Ed.), *The Nebraska Symposium on Motivation, 1989: Cross-cultural perspectives* (Vol. 37, pp. 279–335). Lincoln, NE: University of Nebraska Press.

Colton, C. C. (1829). *Lacon, or, many things in a few words: Addressed to those who think*. New York, NY: C. P. Fessenden.

Connor, K. R., Britton, P. C., Sworts, L. M., & Joiner, T. E. (2007). Suicide attempts among individuals with opiate dependence: The critical role of belonging. *Addictive Behaviors, 32*, 1395–1404.

Costa, P. T., & McCrae, R. R. (1992). *Revised NEO personality inventory (NEO-PI-R) and NEO five-factor inventory (NEO-FFI) manual*. Odessa, FL: Psychological Assessment Resources.

Darbonne, A. R. (1969). Suicide and age: A suicide note analysis. *Journal of Consulting and Clinical Psychology, 33*, 46–50.

Duberstein, P. R., & Conwell, Y. (1997). Personality disorders and completed suicide: A methodological and conceptual review. *Clinical Psychology: Science and Practice, 4*, 359–376.

Ernst, C., Lalovic, A., Lesage, A., Sequi, M., Tousignant, M., & Turecki, G. (2004). Suicide and no axis I psychopathology. *BMC Psychiatry, 4*, 7.

Eysenck, H. J. (1991). Dimensions of personality: 16, 5, or 3?–Criteria for a taxonomic paradigm. *Personality and Individual Differences, 12*, 773–790.

Federal Bureau of Investigation, Behavioral Analysis Unit III. (2010). [Internet Sexual Exploitation of Children (SEOC) Archival Study]. Unpublished raw data.

Finkelhor, D. (1984). How widespread is child sexual abuse? *Children Today, 13*, 18–20.

Foster, T. (2003). Suicide notes themes and suicide prevention. *International Journal of Psychiatry in Medicine, 33*, 323–331.

Gould, M. S., Marrocco, F. A., Kleinman, M., Thomas, J. G., Mostkoff, K., Cote, J. M., & Davies, M. (2005). Evaluating iatrogenic risk of suicide screening programs: A randomized controlled trial. *Journal of the American Medical Association, 293*, 1635–1643.

Gun Control Act of 1968, § 101, Pub. L. No. 90–618, 82 Stat. 1213.

Hall, R. C. W., & Hall, R. C. W. (2007). A profile of pedophilia: Definition, characteristics of offenders, recidivism, treatment outcomes, and forensic issues. *Mayo Clinic Proceedings, 82*, 457–471.

Hall, G. C. N., & Hirschman, R. (1992). Sexual aggression against children: A conceptual perspective of etiology. *Criminal Justice and Behavior, 19*, 8–23.

Hanson, R. K., & Morton-Bourgon, K. E. (2009). The accuracy of recidivism risk assessments for sexual offenders: A meta-analysis of 118 prediction studies. *Psychological Assessment, 21*, 1–21.

Harrington, R., Fudge, H., Rutter, M., Pickles, M., & Hill, J. (1990). Adult outcomes of childhood and adolescent depression. *Archives of General Psychiatry, 47*, 465–473.

Harris, E. C., & Barraclough, B. (1997). Suicide as an outcome for mental disorders. A meta-analysis. *British Journal of Psychiatry, 170*, 205–228.

Hendin, H. (1999). Suicide, assisted suicide, and medical illness. *The Journal of Clinical Psychiatry, 60*, 46–116.

Hepburn, L., Miller, M., Azrael, D., & Hemenway, D. (2007). The U.S. gun stock: Results from the 2004 firearms survey. *Injury Prevention, 13*, 15–19.

Ho, T. P., Yip, P. S. F., Chiu, C. W. F., & Halliday, P. (1998). Suicide notes: What do they tell us? *Acta Psychiatrica Scandinavica, 98*, 467–473.

Hoffer, T., Shelton, J., Behnke, S., & Erdberg, P. (2010). Exploring the impact of child sex offender suicide. *The Journal of Family Violence, 25*, 777–786.

Hoffer, T., Shelton, J., & Joiner, C. (2012). *Operational safety considerations while investigating child sex offenders: A handbook for law enforcement* (Federal Bureau of Investigation, Vol. 1). Washington, DC: Department of Justice.

Howitt, D. (2005). Pornography and the paedophile: Is it criminogenic? *The British Journal of Medical Psychology, 68*, 15–27.

Howitt, D., & Sheldon, K. (2007). The role of cognitive distortion in paedophilic offending: Internet and contact offenders compared. *Psychology, Crime and the Law, 13*, 469–486.

Hull, J., Range, L., & Goggin, W. (1992). Suicide ideas: Relationship to personality disorders on the MCMI. *Death Studies, 16*, 371–375.

Jobes, D. A. (2006). *Managing suicidal risk: A collaborative approach*. New York, NY: The Guilford Press.

Johnson, J., Gooding, P. A., Wood, A. M., & Tarrier, N. (2010). Resilience as positive coping appraisals: Testing the schematic appraisals model of suicide (SAMS). *Behaviour Research and Therapy, 48*, 179–186.

Joiner, T. E. (2005). *Why people die by suicide*. Cambridge, MA: Harvard University Press.

Joiner, T. E. (2010). *Myths about suicide*. Cambridge, MA: Harvard University Press.

Joiner, T. E., Hollar, D., & Van Orden, K. (2006). On Buckeyes, Gators, Super Bowl Sunday, and the Miracle on Ice: 'Pulling together' is associated with lower suicide rates. *Journal of Social and Clinical Psychology, 25*, 179–195.

Joiner, T. E., Pettit, J. W., Walker, R. L., Voelz, Z. R., & Cruz, J. (2002). Perceived burdensomeness and suicidality: Two studies on the suicide notes of those attempting and those completing suicide. *Journal of Social and Clinical Psychology, 21*, 531–545.

Kang, H. K., & Bullman, T. A. (2008). Risk of suicide among US veterans after returning from the Iraq or Afghanistan war zones. *Journal of the American Medical Association, 300*, 652–653.

Kaplan, M. S., Huguet, N., McFarland, B. H., & Newsom, J. T. (2007). Suicide among male veterans: A prospective population-based study. *Journal of Epidemiology and Community Health, 61*, 619–624.

Kehrer, C. A., & Linehan, M. M. (1996). Interpersonal and emotional problem solving skills and parasuicide among women with borderline personality disorder. *Journal of Personality Disorders, 10*, 153–163.

Kellerman, A., Rivara, F., Somes, G., Reay, D., Francisco, J., Banton, J., Prodzinski, J., Fligner, C., & Hackman, B. (1992). Suicide in the home in relation to gun ownership. *The New England Journal of Medicine, 327*, 467–472.

Kessler, R. C. (2000). Some considerations in making resource allocation decisions for the treatment of psychiatric disorders. In G. Andrews & S. Henderson (Eds.), *Unmet need in psychiatry: Problems, resources, responses* (pp. 59–84). Cambridge, UK: Cambridge University Press.

Koren, D., Norman, D., Cohen, A., Berman, J., & Klein, E. M. (2005). Increased PTSD risk with combat-related injury: A matched comparison study of injured and uninjured soldiers experiencing the same combat events. *The American Journal of Psychiatry, 162*, 276–282.

Krafft-Ebbing, R. (1886). *Pyschopathia sexualis*. London, UK: Staples Press.

Kullgren, G., Tengstrown, A., & Grann, M. (1998). Suicide among personality-disordered offenders: A follow-up of 1943 male criminal offenders. *Social Psychiatry and Psychiatric Epidemiology, 33*, S102–S106.

Kung, H. C., Pearson, J. L., & Wei, R. (2005). Substance abuse, firearm availability, depressive symptoms, and mental health utilization among White and African American suicide descendents aged 15 to 64 years. *Annals of Epidemiology, 15*, 614–621.

Kuwabara, H., Shioiri, T., Nishimura, A., Abe, R., Nushida, H., Ueno, Y., Akazawa, K., & Someya, T. (2006). Differences in characteristics between suicide victims who left notes or not. *Journal of Affective Disorders, 94*, 145–149.

Lall, R., Bongar, B., Johnson, B. W., Jain, V. K., & Mittauer, M. W. (1999). Efficacy of the Millon Clinical Multiaxial Inventory-II in discriminating mental health patients with and without suicidal ideation. *Military Psychology, 11*, 423–432.

Lamis, D. A., Langhinrichsen-Rohling, J., & Simpler, A. H. (2008). The associations among personality disorder symptoms, suicide proneness and current distress in adult male prisoners. *Personality and Mental Health, 2*, 218–229.

Lanning, K. V. (2010). *Child molesters: A behavioral analysis*. Alexandria, VA: National Center for Missing and Exploited Children.

Leenaars, A. A. (2004). *Psychotherapy with suicidal people: A person-centered approach*. Hoboken, NJ: Wiley.

Leenaars, A. A., & Balance, W. D. G. (1984). A predictive approach to suicide notes of young and old people from Freud's formulations with regard to suicide. *Journal of Clinical Psychology, 40*, 1362–1364.

Lester, D. (1990). Suicide, homicide, and the quality of life in various countries. *Acta Psychiatrica Scandinavica, 81*, 332–334.

Lester, D. (1999). Gun deaths in children and guns in the home. *European Journal of Psychiatry, 13*, 157–159.

Lester, D., Seiden, R. H., & Tauber, R. K. (1990). Menninger's motives for suicide in genuine, simulated and hoax suicide notes. *Perceptual and Motor Skills, 71*, 248.

Lester, D., Wood, P., Williams, C., & Haines, J. (2004). Motives for suicide: A study of Australian suicide notes. *Crisis, 25*, 33–34.

Linehan, M., Goodstein, J., Nielsen, S., & Chiles, J. (1983). Reasons for staying alive when you are thinking of killing yourself: The reasons for living inventory. *Journal of Consulting and Clinical Psychology, 51*, 276–286.

Linn, M., & Lester, D. (1996). Content differences in suicide notes by gender and age: Serendipitous findings. *Psychological Reports, 78*, 370.

MacLeod, A., Williams, J., & Linehan, M. (1992). New developments in the understanding and treatment of suicidal behaviour. *Behavioural Psychotherapy, 20*, 193–218.

Maris, R. W., Berman, A. L., & Silverman, M. M. (2000). *Comprehensive textbook of suicidology*. New York, NY: The Guilford Press.

Maruschak, L. (2004). *HIV in prisons, 2001* (Bureau of justice statistics bulletin). Washington, DC: U.S. Department of Justice, Office of Justice Programs.

McCann, J. T., & Suess, J. F. (1988). Clinical applications of the MCMI: The 1-2-38- codetype. *Journal of Clinical Psychology, 44*, 181–186.

McClelland, L., Reicher, S., & Both, N. (2000). A last defence: The negotiation of blame within suicide notes. *Journal of Community and Applied Social Psychology, 10*, 225–240.

McIntosh, J. L. (2002). *U.S.A. suicide statistics for the year 1999: Overheads and a presentation guide*. Washington, DC: American Association for Suicidology.

McIntosh, J. L. (2010). *U.S.A. suicide: 2007 Official final data*. Washington, DC: American Association of Suicidology.

Mehrabian, A., & Weinstein, L. (1985). Temperament characteristics of suicide attempters. *Journal of Consulting and Clinical Psychology, 4*, 544–546.

Menninger, K. (1938). *Man against himself*. New York, NY: Harcourt Brace World.

Merriam-Webster. (2004). *Merriam-Webster collegiate dictionary* (11th ed.). Springfield, MA: Author.

Miller, M., Lippman, S. J., Azrael, D., & Hemenway, D. (2007). House firearm ownership and rates of suicide across the 50 United States. *The Journal of Trauma, 62*, 1029–1035.

Miller, J. D., Reynolds, S. K., & Pilkonis, P. A. (2004). The validity of the five-factor model prototypes for personality disorders in two clinical samples. *Psychological Assessment, 16*, 310–322.

Millon, T., Davis, R., Millon, C., & Grossman, S. (2009). *Millon clinical multiaxial inventory-III* (3rd ed.). San Antonio, TX: Pearson.

Millon, T., Millon, C., Davis, R., & Grossman, S. (1997). *The millon clinical multiaxial inventory III (MCMI-III)*. Minneapolis, MN: Pearson Assessments.

Motivans, M. (2007). *Federal prosecution of child sex exploitation offenders, 2006* (Report No. NCJ 219412). Bureau of Justice Statistics Bulletin. Washington, DC: U.S. Department of Justice, Office of Justice Programs.

Murphy, W. D. (1990). Assessment and modification of cognitive distortions in sex offenders. In W. L. Marshall, D. R. Laws, & H. E. Barbaree (Eds.), *Handbook of sexual assault: Issues, theories, and treatment of the offender* (pp. 331–342). New York, NY: Plenum Press.

Ness, D. E., & Pfeffer, C. R. (1986). Sequelae of bereavement resulting from suicide. *The American Journal of Psychiatry, 147*, 279–285.

Nock, M. K., Borges, G., Bromet, E. J., Alonso, J., Angermeyer, M., Beautrais, R., Chiu, W. T., de Girolamo, G., Gluzman, S., de Graaf, R., Gureje, O., Haro, J. M., Huang, Y., Karam, E., Kessler, R. C., Lepine, J. P., Levinson, D., Medina-Mora, M. E., Ono, Y., Posada-Villa, J., & Williams, D. (2008). Cross-national prevalence and risk factors for suicidal ideations, plans, and attempts. *The British Journal of Psychiatry, 191*, 198–205.

Nock, M. K., Borges, G., Bromet, E. J., Cha, C. B., Kessler, R. C., & Lee, S. (2008). Suicide and suicidal behavior. *Epidemiologic Review, 30*, 133–154.

O'Donnell, I., Farmer, R., & Catalan, J. (1993). Suicide notes. *The British Journal of Psychiatry, 163*, 45–48.

Patrick, C. J., Zempolich, K. A., & Levenston, G. K. (1997). Emotionality and violent behavior in psychopaths: A biosocial analysis. In A. Raine, P. A. Brennan, D. P. Farrington, & S. A. Mednick (Eds.), *Biosocial bases of violence* (pp. 145–161). New York, NY: Plenum Press.

Paykel, E. S., Myers, J. K., Lindenthal, J. J., & Tanner, J. (1974). Suicidal feelings in the general population: A prevalence study. *The British Journal of Psychiatry, 124*, 460–469.

Piedmont, R. L. (1998). *The revised NEO personality inventory: Clinical and research applications*. New York, NY: Plenum Press.

Pritchard, C., & Bagley, C. (2000). Multi-criminal and violent groups among child sex offenders: A heuristic typology in a 2-year cohort of 374 men in two English counties. *Child Abuse & Neglect, 24*, 579–586.

Pritchard, C., & King, E. (2005). Differential suicide rates in typologies of child sex offenders in a 6-year consecutive cohort of male suicides. *Archives of Suicide Research, 9*, 35–43.

Quirk, S. W., Christiansen, N. D., Wagner, S. H., & McNulty, J. L. (2003). On the usefulness of measures of normal personality for clinical assessment: Evidence of the incremental validity of the Revised NEO Personality Inventory. *Psychology Assessment, 15*, 311–325.

Ramchand, R., Acosta, J., Burns, R., Jaycox, L., & Pernin, C. (2011). *The war within: Preventing suicide in the U.S. military*. Santa Monica, CA: RAND Corporation.

Roeder, K., Valenstein, M., Forman, J.,Walter, H., Kulkarni, M., & Travis, J. (2009, April). *Acceptability of interventions to delay gun access for VA patients at high risk for suicide.* Paper presented at American Association of Suicidology Annual Conference, San Francisco.

Rossier, J., Meyer de Stadelhofen, F., & Berthoud, S. (2004). The hierarchical structures of the NEO PI-R and the 16 PF 5. *European Journal of Personal Assessment, 20*, 27–38.

Rotter, J. (1966). Generalized expectancies for internal versus external control of reinforcements. *Psychological Monographs, 80*, 609.

Saucier, G., & Goldberg, L. R. (1996). Evidence for the Big Five in analyses of familiar English personality adjectives. *European Journal of Personality, 10*, 61–77.

Schotte, D., & Clum, G. (1987). Problem-solving skills in suicidal psychiatric patients. *Journal of Consulting and Clinical Psychology, 55*, 49–54.

Selby, E. A., Anestis, M. D., Bender, T. W., Riberio, J. D., Nock, M. K., Rudd, M. D., Bryan, C. J., Lim, I. C., Baker, M. T., Gutierrez, P. M., & Joiner, T. E., Jr. (2010). Overcoming the fear of lethal injury: Evaluating suicidal behavior in the military through the lens of the interpersonal-psychological theory of suicide. *Clinical Psychology Review, 30*, 298–307.

Selby, E. A., Anestis, M. D., & Joiner, T. E. (2007). Daydreaming about death: Violent daydreaming as a form of emotion dysregulation in suicidiality. *Behavior Modification, 31*, 867–879.

Seto, M. C. (2008). *Pedophilia and sexual offending against children: Theory, assessment, and intervention*. Washington, DC: American Psychological Association.

Seto, M. C., Hanson, R. K., & Babchishin, K. (2011). Contact sexual offending by men with online sexual offenses. *Sexual Abuse: A Journal of Research and Treatment, 23*, 124–145.

Shneidman, E. (1987). A psychological approach to suicide. In G. R. VandenBos & B. K. Bryant (Eds.), *Cataclysms, crises, and catastrophes: Psychology in action* (pp. 147–183). Washington, DC: American Psychological Association.

Shneidman, E. (1993). *Suicide as psychache: A clinical approach to self-destruction behavior*. New York: Rowman & Littlefield.

Shneidman, E. (1996). *The suicidal mind*. New York: Oxford University Press.

Shneidman, E. (2001). *Comprehending suicide*. Washington, DC: American Psychological Association.

Shneidman, E. S., & Farberow, N. L. (1960). A socio-psychological investigation of suicide. In H. P. David & J. C. Brengelmann (Eds.), *Perspectives in personality research* (pp. 270–293). Oxford, England: Springer.

Silverman, M. M., Bongar, B. M., Berman, A. L., & Maris, R. W. (1999). *Risk management with suicidal patients*. New York, NY: Guilford Press.

SPSS, Inc. (2009). *SPSS Version 190 for Windows*. Chicago, IL: Author.

Stillion, J. M., McDowell, E. E., & May, J. H. (1989). *Suicide across the life span: Premature exits*. New York, NY: Hemisphere.

Strayer, A., & Marzani, G. (2011). Profiles of the offender. In *Suicide by cop: Averting the crisis* (pp. 31–32). Charlottesville, VA: University of Virginia, Critical Incident Analysis Group.

Terr, L. C. (2003). 'Wild Child': How three principles of healing organized 12 years of psychotherapy. *Journal of the American Academy of Child and Adolescent Psychiatry, 42*, 1401–1409.

Thoresen, S., & Mehlum, L. (2006). Suicide in peacekeepers: Risk factors for suicide versus accidental death. *Suicide & Life-Threatening Behavior, 36*, 432–442.

Van Orden, K., Witte, T., Cukrowicz, K., Braithwaite, S., Selby, E., & Joiner, T. (2010). The interpersonal theory of suicide. *Psychological Review, 117*, 575–600.

Van Orden, K. A., Witte, T. K., Gordon, K. H., Bender, T. W., & Joiner, T. E. (2008). Suicidal desire and the capability for suicide: Tests of the interpersonal-psychological theory of suicidal behavior among adults. *Journal of Consulting and Clinical Psychology, 76*, 72–83.

VandenBos, G. R. (2006). *American Psychological Association dictionary of psychology*. Washington, DC: American Psychological Association.

Verona, E., Patrick, C., & Joiner, T. (2001). Psychopathy, antisocial personality, and suicide risk. *Journal of Abnormal Psychology, 110*, 462–70.

Walford, G., Kennedy, M. T., Manwell, M. K., & McCune, N. (1990). Father-perpetrators of child sexual abuse who commit suicide. *Irish Journal of Psychological Medicine, 7*, 144–145.

Ward, T. (2000). Sexual offenders' cognitive distortions as implicit theories. *Aggression and Violent Behavior: A Review Journal, 5*, 491–507.

Ward, T., & Beech, A. (2005). An integrated theory of sexual offending. *Aggression and Violent Behavior: A Review Journal, 11*, 44–63.

Westefield, J., Range, L., Roger, J., Maples, M., Bromley, J., & Alcorn, J. (2000). Suicide: An overview. *The Counseling Psychologist, 28*, 445–510.

Widiger, T. A., & Trull, T. J. (1987). Behavioral indicators, hypothetical constructs, and personality disorders. *Journal of Personality Disorders, 1*, 82–87.

Wild, N. J. (1998). Suicide of perpetrators after disclosure of child sexual abuse. *Child Abuse & Neglect, 12*, 119–121.

Wilson, G. D., & Cox, D. N. (1983). Personality of paedophile club members. *Personality and Individual Differences, 4*, 323–329.

Wolak, J., Finkelhor, D., & Mitchell, K. J. (2004). Internet-initiated sex crimes against minors: Implications for prevention based on findings from a national study. *The Journal of Adolescent Health, 35*, 424–433.

Woods, P. J., Silverman, E. S., Gentilini, J. M., Cunningham, D. K., & Grieger, R. M. (1991). Cognitive variables related to suicide contemplation in adolescents with implications for long range prevention. *Journal of Rational-Emotive & Cognitive-Behavior Therapy, 9*, 215–245.

Worden, J. W. (1996). *Children and grief: When a parent dies*. New York, NY: Guilford Press.

Yates, M. T. (2012). *The reliability and validity of the general assessment questionnaire revised: An operational measure of personality factors*. (Unpublished doctoral dissertation). Gallaudet University, Washington, DC.

Index

T.A. Hoffer and J.L.E. Shelton, *Suicide Among Child Sex Offenders*, SpringerBriefs in Psychology, DOI 10.1007/978-1-4614-5937-8,

© Springer Science+Business Media New York 2013

Acknowledgments

The authors would like to thank the BAU staff who assisted with this project: Research Coordinator Yvonne Muirhead; Unit Chief Terri Patterson; Supervisory Special Agents (SSAs) James Beasley, William Donaldson, Adrienne Isom, Kristen Slater, and Michael Yoder; Intelligence Analysts Jessica Owens and Colleen Hyland; Office Support Specialist Rebecca Ross; and Research Analyst Adrienne Hoffman-Lewis. Additionally, the authors appreciate the thoughts and ideas of former and current FBI and law enforcement personnel: Retired SSA Jennifer Eakin; SSA Kathleen Canning; Unit Chief of Violent Crimes/Crimes Against Children Intelligence Unit Kevin Gutfleish; Chief Division Counsel Kenneth Gross; and Detective Mary J. Anders, Montgomery County, PA District Attorney's Office; as well as the law enforcement officers and agents who shared information and insights with us. Finally, the authors would like to express appreciation to the members of the BAU's Behavioral Research Working Group, along with Thomas Joiner, Ph.D., Florida State University; David Jobes, Ph.D., Catholic University; Alan Berman, Ph.D., American University, and especially the family members and friends who took the time to share their thoughts and feelings about their loved ones.

T.A. Hoffer and J.L.E. Shelton, *Suicide Among Child Sex Offenders*,
SpringerBriefs in Psychology, DOI 10.1007/978-1-4614-5937-8,
© Springer Science+Business Media New York 2013

MIX
Papier aus verantwortungsvollen Quellen
Paper from responsible sources
FSC® C105338

If you have any concerns about our products,
you can contact us on
ProductSafety@springernature.com

In case Publisher is established outside the EU,
the EU authorized representative is:
Springer Nature Customer Service Center GmbH
Europaplatz 3, 69115 Heidelberg, Germany

Printed by Libri Plureos GmbH
in Hamburg, Germany